Feel Free

The behaviour m٤
guide for new tea៴៸៴៸៴

Nikki Cunningham-Smith

BLOOMSBURY EDUCATION

LONDON OXFORD NEW YORK NEW DELHI SYDNEY

BLOOMSBURY EDUCATION
Bloomsbury Publishing Plc
50 Bedford Square, London, WC1B 3DP, UK
29 Earlsfort Terrace, Dublin 2, Ireland

BLOOMSBURY, BLOOMSBURY EDUCATION and the Diana logo are trademarks
of Bloomsbury Publishing Plc

First published in Great Britain, 2021

A catalogue record for this book is available from the British Library

ISBN: PB: 978-1-4729-8448-7; ePDF: 978-1-4729-8450-0;
ePub: 978-1-4729-8449-4

2 4 6 8 10 9 7 5 3 1 (paperback)

Typeset by Newgen KnowledgeWorks Pvt. Ltd., Chennai, India
Printed and bound in the UK by CPI Group Ltd, CR0 4YY

MIX
Paper from
responsible sources
FSC® C013604

To find out more about our authors and books visit www.bloomsbury.com
and sign up for our newsletters

For Sam, Illyanna and Xanthe

Contents

Acknowledgements

Firstly, to my awesome husband Sam. I don't think words will justify how much of my other half he is, even in those moments of stress when I don't show it. Thank you for knowing just from a look when I need you more. Thank you for making me laugh but also making me feel like the most accomplished and successful woman, even before I have accomplished anything or proven my success. I love you. Let's keep laughing into our next adventure.

To my amazing parents Carl and Des for always asking, 'What's next?', so I could and would never rest on my laurels, but also for making sure nothing ever felt out of my reach or capabilities. They led by example of what a strong work ethic is and told me that they will always be boastful about me behind my back and never to my face. I don't know why but I love that sentiment. My biggest secret cheerleaders. I love you both and thank you for everything you've done for me and my family.

Thank you to my wonderful in-laws Julia and Colin for supporting us in so many ways, never hesitating to have our tiny human and entertaining her on those days when the deadlines loomed. For providing the Tenby holiday and the time for an hour's break from being a new mum to reengage my brain cells and develop the proposal for this book. I love and appreciate all you do for our little family.

To all of the wonderful educators who took the time to offer their stories, especially during a time of navigating a new landscape of teaching, with blended learning, and balancing your own physical and mental health and fears. Thank you for the love and passion you have for educating the future, especially in recent months when teaching has been so difficult. I dedicate the chapter 'So... you're wondering why we need you to stay' to all of you wonderful people.

To the first person who believed I had an interesting writing voice, Jon Severs, who regularly commissioned my words (even though I sometimes couldn't understand why), and to Hannah Marston who received the proposal for this book, saw something in it and supported me in growing and nurturing it into the book you have today.

To all my friends both in and out of education, who kept being a reassuring voice in my ear, at whatever stage of my career, and who were positive voices when writing during lockdown and the first trimester, and the feat seemed bigger than me (I'm looking at you, Anna Johnson-Thorpe, Nessa Ward, Vic Raynor, Kay Humphrey, Dominique Evans, Tetters, Jen Marscheider, Heather Tucker, Serena Rivers and Shelly Hurrell). And to Kathy Balebela and Andy Laker, my ITT mentors whose advice I still hold close today.

To my darling Illyana, my daughter on the outside. This book was conceived whilst I was on maternity leave with you, in those moments of quiet and cuddles that you just don't get when the world is going at 100 mph. Your playroom became my office, and in our shared pandemic space you were my only co-worker but welcome company. Thank you for keeping up your Friday naps so that I could write in that time but most importantly for teaching me to find humour and seek fresh air when everything feels too hard.

To Xanthe, my daughter on the inside. At the point of writing this, you are still a wriggling companion, our own little team of two-in-one, keeping me on my toes, battling tiredness and nausea, my constant companion for this whole book writing process, giving me a well-needed kick (literally) when I've needed it, reminding me that I'm doing this to set an example to my daughters, my future Queens.

And to anyone who has been told that you need to work twice as hard for half the reward, keep plugging, keep banging down the doors to occupy the space, because you deserve to be there just as much as anyone.

Introduction

They may say never to work with animals and children, but when you see the joy, creativity, fun and downright hilarity that children can bring about in your daily life, I'm sure you'll join me in disagreeing with that sentiment. Teaching is an amazing career. No two days are ever the same and each lesson brings with it many rewarding and uplifting moments. But, like in every job, with those highs do come some lows, and bad behaviour may seem like one of those areas where you keep coming unstuck time and time again.

Although there are always a huge number of factors that can contribute to a person leaving the teaching profession, it cannot be ignored that a large contributor, especially among newly qualified teachers (NQTs), is the behaviour of pupils. While teachers are professionals, it is important to remember that we are mere mortals – even though it may feel at times that the requirement that is missed out on our job specification is to be superhuman. As teachers, we are often put in a position where we feel like we are getting it wrong multiple times a day. A reset starts when the bell goes or when the next lesson transition occurs. This can either bring about an exoneration from a lesson gone wrong, or it can continue our spiral towards feeling inadequate. Some teachers have the ability to dust themselves off and try again. Some have skin thicker than a rhinoceros, so regardless of what has happened, it will have no effect on their demeanour or outcomes. But there is a good majority who will take it to heart. They may even take it further and end up in a place where they feel like they have failed not just as a teacher, but as a person. This state of mind can have a detrimental effect on one's ability to teach and one's mental wellbeing. After all, if you spend the majority of your time in an environment where you are made to feel inferior, you will begin to believe that you are.

Now more than ever, we need to find ways to make sure that those amazing human beings who are entering our wonderful profession (like you!) choose to remain, and also choose to remain for the right reasons! We need to make sure that there is a culture of support, no matter what school you are in, and that there is an opportunity to ask for help to improve your own personal practices, through modelling, coaching and CPD. I want teachers to be able to reach out and ask for help if they're struggling with behaviour, without it feeling like it will go as a strike against your name, or be used against you at a later date. I want you – and all NQTs – to know that it's OK and perfectly normal to struggle with behaviour, particularly at the start of your career. It isn't about you being a bad teacher or 'not cut out for the job'. You need to collect and practise a range of skills and strategies for successful behaviour management. Handling bad behaviour in the classroom is not something that's inherent in your personality, rather it's something you can – and will – develop and improve over time.

Most importantly to me, there needs to be scope to find humour in the horror! As in life, nothing is prescribed, and sometimes the best-laid plans are the ones that are just as likely to go wrong. If there was one sentiment that got me through my initial years in teaching, it was the lyrics from a song that said, 'I will find strength in pain', as sometimes my lessons were painful, but the strength that I was able to take from them was the ability to be a reflective practitioner: to understand what had happened and think about what I could do differently next time. But more than anything, it was the ability to talk to my colleagues, get support and laugh at some of my most monumental mess-ups. It is not lost on me how many comedians have a background in teaching. You are, in essence, in the league of stand-up every day. Ready to be respected or heckled, ready with a cheeky retort to keep that stage sailing smoothly and your audience hanging on every word. With this in mind, I want to help you develop a mindset that is indicative to humour, not taking yourself seriously all the time and creating a safe, reflective space to help you improve your practice.

How I hope this book will help you

This book will consider a series of common scenarios related to challenging behaviour in the classroom, from completely losing control of a lesson, to being outsmarted by the class clown. These scenarios are experienced every day by teachers up and down the country. If they happen to you, there really is no reason to be mortified and think that teaching isn't the right career for you. Instead, your focus should be on reflecting about what happened and developing some tactics to deal with the same situation next time. I hope the book will become a space where you do not feel ashamed of the moments that went awry and where you can instead look back at these moments with fondness and the occasional red face. For each behaviour scenario presented, I offer a set of practical strategies for you to choose between, based on the needs of your pupils. And spoiler alert: 'not smiling before Christmas' isn't one of them! You should practise the strategies you feel are most relevant for the next time you're faced with a similar situation, to boost your confidence and ensure you're ready to handle it.

I bring along with us for the ride thoughts from other educational practitioners: those who have been in their post for years and bring with it wisdom, and also some newbies who are just starting out with their fresh concepts and ideas. I hope these contributors will demonstrate to you that all teachers are experiencing the same scenarios as you and I hope that what you will have in front of you are cracking tales of resilience, reflection and moments of 'Really? Did that just happen?!'

With these two unique perspectives, it's incredibly important for you to understand that there are some stereotypes attributed to teachers when it comes to years of service. For example, if you've been practising for a long time, you are an oracle but you are also more cynical, with PTSD-esque flashbacks because, 'You haven't seen the things that I've seen, man!' Or, if you are fresh into the teaching sphere, you are so doe-eyed and optimistic that you don't know anything and are absolutely not yet equipped to contribute towards educational dialogue on any topic, let alone behaviour, especially as I definitely saw you smiling in front of your class the other day and it's only October... you fool! Both of these stereotypes have the potential to be damaging when we start to think of ways to promote an open and honest dialogue around behaviour. All inputs and opinions are incredibly relevant if we are to work on the joint outcome of providing exceptional educational opportunities for our learners whilst also supporting colleagues and our own sanity, helping us stay motivated, and most importantly, one step ahead of those most likely to derail our lessons.

Running alongside all this, I'll take you on a whistle-stop tour of the research that is out there to back up the practice with the theory (because I am a teacher after all and every day is a school day!). While this element won't be too weighty, it will be useful for you to see that these behavioural issues are being looked at across the globe, with varying conclusions and suggested practices.

The words that I share with you are my take-homes and opinions about how to deal with commonly found classroom scenarios related to behaviour. I'm forever grateful for the behaviour books that I read in my early career, but I always thought that I was a buffoon in the classroom, as the situations that were presented in them did not seem to be realistic to me. Why was I the only one who, after explaining the task and asking the class if they had any questions, had a pupil raise their hand and say, 'Miss, why were you buying so much chocolate so late last night in Asda? Couldn't you have sent your boyfriend to go and get it?' (More on this in Chapter 1…) With that in mind, I hope this book presents to you some realistic scenarios you might come across in the classroom, along with practical advice on what to do to get your lesson back on track – and to get you and your pupils smiling again!

Chapter 1

So... you're wondering why we need you to stay

In the last 12 years, I have had the fortune to work in a multitude of jobs throughout secondary education. Straight out of university, I got my first job temping as a teaching assistant (TA) in an inner-city school in Nottingham, and quite frankly I was hooked. It was one of the toughest jobs that I've ever had. The free school meals percentage was high, and when completing data, it was almost easier to tick who wasn't EAL (English as an additional language) and PP (pupil premium). While the building was amazing, the personal lives of the majority of our pupils were not. And yet, teachers rocked up day after day in the most challenging of work environments, and delivered to those pupils the best they knew how. It was a tough environment, and I realised just how tough it was when I attended my first end-of-term staff debrief and realised that there were over 20 teaching staff leaving, and of those, some were even leaving the profession altogether. My mind boggled. This was my first experience of being in a school through my own choice and I loved going to that job so much. It shocked me to think that this very same school environment was driving some teachers away.

Though there were challenges, and lots of them, some of those pupils were the most hilarious humans that I had ever (and still have ever) come across. The camaraderie of the staff was binding and kept us all working towards the same goal, even if it seemed at the time that that goal was to get to the pub on Friday after school for our own personal debriefs, rather than the one led by the senior leadership team (SLT). An SLT that would join us on occasion to take part in the cathartic release of the week's trials and tribulations. My experience as a TA was not the same as that of the teachers, but I got to hear a lot of incidents that had taken place from a lot of different viewpoints: the teachers' (both sober and tipsy!), the pupils' (don't worry, they weren't in the pub with us – their pub was down the road), and sometimes, when I had been there to see what had actually taken place, my own. I often had my own professional (and oh so naive at times) opinion on the matter. But one thing that I always took from the interactions was the teachers' passion that was tinged with frustration of wanting to do the best job possible, but just not being able to. Hands were tied by the constraints of the teaching environment, whether that be resources, parental engagement, lesson planning or changing of exam specifications. But the one recurring topic, which seemed to be a decider in how these amazing people saw themselves as educators in the classroom, was behaviour. Both in and out of the classroom.

Certain names would be a recurring theme for the topic of conversation, and what fascinated me the most was that one of these pupils happened to be in all of the same lessons as the pupil I was supporting in my TA role. On a daily basis, I could watch this pupil transform from a willing participator, engaged in learning, and a caring member of the class, to someone who was hell bent on disrupting, disengaging and taking others along for the ride of no learning. The only thing that remained constant was the teachers who were being affected negatively by his behaviour, continually working to try and change his actions so they wouldn't disrupt learning. I was also seeing some staff feeling it was a personal attack on them when another colleague would utter those fatal words, 'Oh, he behaves for me.' I remember there was one teacher who felt so victimised that, at the end-of-term debrief, she let us know she would be leaving teaching to 'work with people who would listen to her'. All I could think of was how amazing her lessons had been, and how if I'd had her teach me when I was at school, I may have actually been interested in that subject. I wondered why she couldn't see what I (and the majority of her class) could see.

Since then, I have made it my own personal mission to champion incredible colleagues who have felt that they are less than good, particularly because of challenging classroom behaviours. I have coached in schools to offer this support to try and engage with staff to make them see that some small tweaks can enable them to stay. Introducing a reflective practitioner approach often allows them to be able to see this. And it's this exact same thing that I want to share with you in this book.

But before we start, I want to explore a little more the reasons why bad classroom behaviour is chasing so many new teachers away from the profession, explain why we really need *you* to stick with us, and offer a few practical strategies that might just make all the difference.

Why is bad behaviour causing teachers to quit?

In March 2018, the Department for Education published some interesting research into why teachers were leaving the profession. The researchers interviewed 80 primary and secondary teachers about the reasons they believed were key in influencing decisions to quit. Many reasons were cited, from workload to accountability, but the issue of behaviour came up time and time again. The findings relevant to behaviour included the following:

- The teachers interviewed believed greater levels of support and understanding from the SLT were needed, for example, in terms of the management of pupil behaviour, and the ability to have open and honest conversations. This would help support teachers' relationships with their SLT and reduce feelings of pressure in terms of scrutiny, accountability and workload.
- Teachers found it difficult to be creative in their planning and teaching, due to being hindered by time or challenges around pupil behaviour.
- Commonly, teachers had been aspirational (some referred to themselves as 'idealistic') before entering the profession and felt that they would be:
  - 'Firm but fair'.
  - Approachable – the type of teacher that young people can turn to for advice.
  - Able to motivate pupils and make a difference.
  They often mentioned wanting to emulate the example of a good teacher they had known during their own schooling – inspiring young people and engaging them with a subject.
- Although a small number (five) had anticipated some pupil behavioural issues, they had expected that they would be 'respected' as

teachers. However, when in the role, some perceived that this was not always the case.

- Teachers commonly reported the 'high' of seeing young people make progress or connect with a subject, such as a lesson that they felt had gone well and where pupils demonstrated that they had understood the content. The attitude of pupils had a large influence on these teachers; where young people were motivated to learn or were enthusiastic, teachers reported that this increased their positivity towards their role. Where there were disciplinary issues, this proved challenging in terms of maintaining an effective lesson, but also created additional workload when communicating with parents or carers and logging behavioural issues on a central system. A small number had enjoyed the challenge of working with pupils with complex behavioural issues, to help support them and make a difference.

- Early career teachers made the decision to leave the profession much more quickly than more experienced teachers. Generally, their reasons for leaving the profession did not differ compared to more experienced teachers. However, they were more likely to report that they found poor pupil behaviour difficult to manage.

Adapted from Department for Education (2018)

It doesn't make it very difficult to see that there is a clear link between the reasons that teachers leave our profession and the behaviour of pupils. Studies are repeatedly showing this factor coming out in several forms, whether that be the personal emotions related to struggling with behaviour or not feeling supported by the systems and structures around them (the behaviour management policies, middle and senior leadership, the parents and the local community). It's disheartening to see that early career teachers are more likely to exit the profession due to behaviour, but it's also understandable. Resilience to a situation is something that is built up over time, and if the expectations of a scenario are not what you are expecting, it can be quite a shock to the system. Sitting on Twitter a few weeks into September, you can see the cries for help ringing out from NQTs:

- 'I've just had a hellish lesson, I don't know if this is for me.'
- 'I forgot everything. I feel so stupid.'

- 'Thank God it's Friday. I can hide with this glass of wine for the next few days and think about school never.'

- '#HELP'

Supportive measures can be hard to come by if you feel scared to articulate that you are struggling at any stage of your career, especially if you fear repercussions such as pay progression being affected or a stigma being attached to you as not being seen as one of the school's 'good' teachers. Whether we care to admit that it is part of the narrative in schools, it is there: a secret league table, and not wanting to be the one who lets the side down, especially if there are any visitors to your classroom that day.

I am a big believer in transparency and honesty when it comes to making progress. Support begins from knowing the areas that need to be focused on to move forward, and once this has been identified, sensible, practical and pragmatic steps need to be put in place. A removal of some of the negative culture that can be associated with behaviour management is a helpful place to begin.

How to fall in love with teaching, despite bad behaviour

At this point, I think it would be great to hear from our first early-career contributor, fresh out of the blocks on a journey that will hopefully lead to many happy and fruitful years as an educator. Fresh-faced and ready to get the metaphorical dust on him from being at the chalkface, Stefan will take a look at what could impact new teachers in their formative years in terms of behaviour and reassure us that it's far from being all bad news.

Case study: Stefan Hines, NQT

I have taught for almost two years now and it is safe to say there have been many challenges as well as rewards! While it is one of the hardest careers I've faced, the rewards by far make it all worthwhile. If nothing else, it imprints a plethora of stories that you'll be telling for years to come about the impact you made on a child's life that day. As a science teacher, I feel that opportunity is even more present, and one example of this is when teaching the topic of reproduction! I've taught this topic several times now to both Years 7 and 8, and the results are somewhat astonishing. Despite covering topics that are a little nerve-wracking for a new teacher, I have experienced heightened interest and brilliant classroom behaviour on all occasions... even when a Year 8 girl exclaimed to the class, 'Wait... what? We have two holes down there?!' Another girl approached me at the end of a lesson, horrified, to thank me for ruining her favourite song earlier that lesson when she asked, 'Sir, what happens when the sperm meets the egg?' I openly replied to the class, 'Well, think of it like the Spice Girl's song "When 2 Become 1". They fuse together and start dividing!' She also continued to tell me how she was off home to tell her parents that she now understands how babies are made, as 'it's gross'.

But as well as the funny moments, my teaching of this topic gave students the opportunity to understand themselves and ask questions in a safe space. One moment that always sticks in my mind was when a regularly disruptive student came to me at the end of the lesson and asked, 'So, you know you said in puberty it's common to have mood swings, is that why I feel angry quite often?' Giving him a deeper understanding of the changes teenagers experience helped him to understand why he perhaps felt particular emotions. Each lesson should always teach students something new. Occasionally, it may even teach them something about themselves.

Reflecting on why an effective behaviour for learning environment was achieved when teaching such topics, I think it's extremely clear: the students were engaged, they were interested, and I was confident in my delivery. I believe that my students were engaged in this topic simply because it was so relevant to them; students must have a reason to engage with learning, and one surefire way of getting their attention is by making it relevant. This can be achieved by discussing where topics fit into real life, and why the information you're about to teach them will be useful and help them in the long run. This is a principle I have fully taken on board, and at the start of lessons I regularly discuss with students what the point of the lesson is, and how and why it is relevant to them. No exam talk, no assessment objectives. Just relevance. In my experience, there is a clear correlation between relevance, engagement and behaviour.

I also fully understand that some of the content in this particular topic may have felt embarrassing to students; this made me ensure that I tackled the topic with a confident yet relaxed approach. When teaching, your own emotions and body language are significant; if you are talking about something with confidence, the students will respond to that; they will believe what you are saying and want to learn more. By taking a semi-relaxed approach with students, it allows for effective relationships built on respect. This creates a safe space for learning, in which students feel comfortable and therefore engaged. The implementation of such thought processes and strategies across the board has helped me to deliver some of the best lessons I've had, regardless of topic! Relationships, relevance and confidence in delivery will secure desired behaviours in most scenarios.

So, what's the point in all this? Well, as much as the government and the rest of the country need us to keep teaching in schools, in the past two years it has become exceptionally clear to me that there is no greater need to keep at it than for the children themselves. The relationships you build in teaching are by far the greatest reward I have experienced from any career.

Stefan Hines is a secondary science teacher about to start his NQT year.

These words from Stefan highlight to me that we all enter teaching with the passion and determination we need to keep us coming back. I have never found a thought process more inaccurate than when I have had the phrase 'Those who can't, teach' uttered to me in jest, because those who can't, really don't teach. A passion for the subject alone is not one that usually draws people towards teaching. We are in the business of children and all the sticky tricky extras that come with it. And that is why I believe it must be a heavy heart and a lot of soul-destroying decisions that lead someone to leave. But that thought process is far from the be-all-and-end-all. In my opinion, teaching is in fact a bit of a calling. You didn't take the decision to apply for whichever route you went down and endure a year of training only for you to think this is totally not for you. I believe that any trainee teacher who successfully completes their training year has an extra hidden vat of resilience that isn't handed out to mere mortals, so kudos to you for tapping into it. And if you feel you haven't yet, I hope the behaviour management playbook will begin to tap into that resource on your behalf. You're welcome!

The behaviour management playbook

Being able to teach is as much about being able to impart knowledge as being able to develop a multi-disciplinary approach to controlling the environment that you need to command on a day-to-day basis. But as with any situation, sometimes the best-laid plans can still go awry. This is where I tell everyone that it is incredibly important for you to develop an arsenal of tactics. I personally do not think that it is overkill to have five to ten behaviour management options to hand for every lesson, tailored to the needs of the class that you are working with. While this may seem like a sizeable number, it doesn't necessarily mean that you would be using them all in one go. In fact, I would suggest the opposite.

I call this having a **playbook**. I have taken this concept from my knowledge as a basketball and netball coach. In every game situation, you need to be able to assess and prescribe an outcome quickly before the outcome can get too far out of control. Sometimes, on the spot, creativity can come into play to combat the problem presented, but other times your brain is not going to be able to react quickly enough, and that's why you have a playbook. Have you ever watched *The Waterboy* where the coach was nothing without his playbook and the other coach became the legend because he stole the ideas in it? If so, you'll know exactly what I mean.

If there is a player who is taking all the shots without being challenged, then I (the coach) have three options of 'plays' to direct to the players. If the first doesn't work, I have the choice of being able to cycle through the other options. Not only are these well versed by me, but the team I'm coaching are aware of the plays too, meaning that with all the practice sessions we go through, these plays are now muscle memory, triggered by a visual or auditory command.

This practice can be taken on when in your classroom space, especially in your formative teaching years, or when you have been entered into a new scenario, like a new school or a new class at the start of the academic year. Formulate a series of 'plays' based on the behavioural needs of your pupils that you can cycle through as and when required. If one doesn't work, try the next and then the next. And remember to train your pupils so they know and understand these plays and can use them to self-regulate too. While the advice once was 'Don't smile until Christmas', I have always taken the stance of 'Train them Term 1'. By training, I mean get them used to your way of working and your classroom expectations. This is where my favourite psychological theory comes into play (yes, I have favourites, and if you keep researching pupil behaviour throughout your career, so will you): Pavlov's Dogs. If you aren't *au fait* with this particular theory, a quick whistlestop is that Pavlov managed to get his dogs salivating just by ringing a bell, through a series of steps of reward and food association whenever a bell was rung. It meant that through a positive interaction or experience, the dogs were able to carry out a task with no prompts from Pavlov but instead by being triggered by a stimulus.

An example of how I would use this in my classroom practice would be to get my pupils used to hearing a certain piece of music whenever I would want them to start to tidy up. In September, I would turn on the music and simultaneously instruct them of the steps that they need to perform: 'Save your work with a good file name; close your applications down; wipe down your mouse and keyboard; place the keyboard under the screen; return the monitor to its lowest height; put the mouse next to the keyboard; hang up your headphones; pass any papers to the end of your row; person at the end, bring the papers from your row to the front; tuck your chairs in; stand behind your chairs quietly.'

Over time, I would remove some instructions until we were left with me just putting on the music. What would start as a melee of activity and noise in September would become a calm activity by October or November, and all just by turning on a piece of music. Even the choice of music would help them understand how much time they had: classical pieces if we had time to flow with it all, the *Benny Hill* theme if they needed to crack on! Throughout the year I would do reminder sessions of my expectations, key times being after a holiday or after a lesson when they may not have got it right.

Unfortunately, some settings would not agree on sacrificing some of your learning time to work on this. However, I personally advocate it wherever possible and find it essential for minimising disruption, giving you more learning time and boosting pupil progress in the long run.

In each chapter of this book, you'll find a set of 'plays' for your playbook relating to the scenario being discussed. So, for this first chapter, here are some initial 'plays' that aim to help you avoid a situation where bad behaviour threatens to overwhelm you and that will help you focus on the positives of the job rather than the challenges of classroom management.

Plays for the playbook

Be kind to yourself and think about why you might be struggling

The main tip I'm going to offer on this topic is that you need to be kind and honest with yourself, and realise that you are human. Every teacher will have experienced similar struggles, especially in their NQT year, so you are not alone. If you are finding negative feelings are a regular occurrence, ask the question about who is making you feel this way. What are the contributing factors that are making you feel like this? Do you feel confident in asking for additional support, or do you feel that it will be used against you so you choose to struggle on?

Is the setting you're in the right one for you, not just in terms of the exact school, but key stage, independent, state or specialist? Are you teaching in your area of passion or are you filling a spot in your school? Are you planning your days and your lessons, or are you winging it all the time? Is your marking up to date, or are you living in fear of a book scrutiny? How is your overall time management? Are you in teaching for the wage, for the subject knowledge or for the pupil interactions? (I see nothing wrong with any of those reasons, but you need to know why you're here, else it will make it even harder to stay on a bad day if none of these reasons are fulfilled.)

Some genuine soul-searching and asking of difficult questions will help put yourself in a position where you may find a change is the answer rather than an exit. I know that I for one would be grateful if we could figure out a way to make you stay.

Create your own playbook

Through reading more books like this, visiting and observing other schools and other types of settings, you will hopefully be in a position where you can nab ideas and add them to your playbook. When I'm visiting another school, I particularly love taking a look on their walls or inside their classrooms to see if there is anything that I can add to my own ever-expanding playbook. Your playbook may be in your head, or (as in my case), it may be a battered notebook that is always at hand to jot down ideas. If you don't have one, start to create your own. You can use the plays in this book as a starting point for making your very own list of strategies that might work. And share the love by letting others see yours and contributing to theirs.

Find your village to help you stay

I'm hoping this book goes some way to helping with this. The case studies in this book may trigger you when you are struggling and serve as a reminder that you are not an island and support is there in many guises. If you have a BTF (best teacher friend) or a work hubby or wife, like I've always had, then you never need to have that feeling of being an island. An island of solitude can make you think that you have the worst behaviour management in the world and that no one else is in the same boat. Having a village around you will help keep your mental wellbeing strong when tackling questions of behaviour that you may have, providing sounding boards and signposting opportunities. Here are some reasons why a BTF or work husband or wife is essential in any school:

- You never have to eat lunch off your lap in the toilet to avoid being alone – they'll be in the cubicle next to you, standing over the top calling you names.
- You will never be late. Yeah, you're running ten minutes late for a staff briefing, and the head's spotted this, but your BTF/H/W will make up some excuse that will not only exonerate you, but will make you look epic in the meantime, e.g. 'Oh yes, she's dealing with a feral parent in reception.'
- You will never have to worry about forgetting your lunch. You are so indebted to each other because you have bought each other snacks on umpteen occasions, and somehow you have synchronised your wallets so that no matter who forgets their scran, there is always food money or a chocolate fund to go round.

- Your cup never runneth dry. Neither of you will dare to be the first to commit the cardinal sin of not getting the other a brew. No matter what part of the school you're in, they will automatically make your strong coffee with one and half sugars.

- You'll never have a bad day. Because even if you do, they'll have your back. People will not dare bitch about you when they are in the vicinity because no one wants this tag team coming to take them down. They pick you up when you're low, they'll laugh with you when you messed up a lesson, they'll tell you to 'fess up when you're in the wrong. They'll remind you when a report or data drop is due and tell you when your vest top is too low. They'll defend you to the kids, big you up to parents and have a sneaky tipple on a residential (no teacher does that… honest). But most of all, they will answer an SOS text any time to reassure you that yes, you are in fact a numpty, now go to sleep.

If you find that you don't have this available to you in your current setting, there are many online networking opportunities, including via Twitter hashtags. Examples include: #ukedchat #edchat #edteach #education #edu #elearning #ks1 #ks2 #ks3 #ks4 #earlyyears #EYFS #nqtchat #NQT #teachertips #teaching #SEN #edutwitter #teachers #pastoraledchat #SEMHchat #sendhelp #thisisAP #BAMEed #LGBTed #MTPTproject #MTPTchat #womened #edumtp #tinyvoicetalks #PGCE #ALN to name a few. There are often events that may cater to your networking needs too, such as BrewEd, WomenEd, BAMEed, Young Black Teachers Network, LGBTed and Maternity CPD, where you might find people you can identify with and spaces where you are comfortable sharing your experiences. Schools in your local authority or multi-academy trust may also have groups for networking opportunities, inclusive of ITTs, NQTs, middle leaders, senior leaders, pastoral leaders and subject specific, so keep your eye out for them too.

Use the playbook scenarios and reflective spaces in this book

When a frankly mortifying behavioural situation happens to you, the first thing you want to do is go home, have a glass of wine and pretend it never happened. But wait! Next time you're faced with a behavioural incident, instead of trying to force your brain to forget about it (which is pretty much impossible, by the way), take a moment to reflect on it. However painful this is right now, it will be beneficial in the long run, I promise. Reflect on why the incident occurred and what you can do to get a plan ready for next time (because there will be a next time, and it'll be when you least expect it!). Each of the chapters that follow will present to you some behaviour scenarios that have genuinely happened to NQTs or experienced teachers. For each chapter, it's well worth taking the time to think of a similar incident that you yourself have experienced and answer the following series of questions:

1. What happened?
2. Was this experience personal?
3. How did the incident make you feel?
4. Is there a repeat offender involved in the situation?
5. Were there any catalysts or red flags to the incident?
6. Have you decided to take any additional steps (e.g. call home, detention, involving another member of staff)?
7. Do you feel like leaving the classroom? Why?
8. What's one thing that you would do differently if the same situation were to arise?

I've left a reflective space at the end of each chapter in the book for you to answer these questions and write notes that you can refer back to time and again.

An example

I thought that for the first chapter, I would give you a scenario that has happened to me as an example and I'll answer the playbook questions in relation to it. That way, you can see how you can use this space (because we teachers love to model, don't we, or else how on earth am I going to get you to achieve?!).

I mentioned in the introduction the lesson where, when I asked the class if there were any questions before starting a task, a pupil came out with: 'Miss, why were you buying so much chocolate so late last night in Asda? Couldn't you have sent your boyfriend to go and get it?' Let me tell you a bit more about what happened next...

Having been completely wrong-footed, as this clearly was not a question on how to program a loop in Python, without thinking, my quick mouth responded with: 'Some advice, Ben. If you see a woman in a shop that late at night with an armful of chocolate, it's safe to say there's no boyfriend at home.' Immediately I became crippled with anxiety. Had I just overshared? Had I just unintentionally reinforced a negative stereotype? Where did he even see me? Why was *he* out so late? Did I now need to talk to the designated safeguarding lead (DSL)? Did I need to move house? Did I really need to buy *that* much chocolate? And why had I eaten it all, as I would clearly need some when I got home tonight after this very awkward exchange? And more importantly, how did I now regain control of the giggling class that I may have inadvertently put off task all by myself?!

I flapped and ultimately lost the class, only for my head of department to poke his head around the door and (though he smiled at me) he took one look at my class and they were silenced. He saved my bacon that day, but I couldn't help walking away from that lesson feeling like an imposter, a fraud and totally incompetent, as it had taken someone else to keep my class in check. If I could pop my head around the door of my classroom ten years ago in that situation, I would hang about and past me and present me would laugh it off together. At the time, I stewed on it that night and for the next few weeks until my NQT review when I was sure it would come back to bite me and I would be kicked out of the teaching profession for good with a shame bell ringing behind me as I left. It didn't happen. And I'm sure my old head of department has no recollection of the incident, and yet, here I am, writing it in the opening of my book to you, as this incident was one of the many that has shaped my outlook and practice in behaviour. Had I taken the many incidents completely to heart, I don't think I would have felt completely able to stay in teaching. Ultimately, I stayed because the highs far outweighed the lows. The challenges that were thrown my way weren't always such game changers that I couldn't come back from them, and ultimately, there was never a day when I couldn't find a little glimmer of hope. Whether that be a pupil finally nailing a concept, or being on break duty and a child making me laugh, there was always a moment I could find that would keep me going. That, and I always knew deep down how much I loved this job and the staff and pupils I got to work with.

So, how would I answer the reflective questions about this scenario? Here goes:

1. What happened?

See above...

2. Was this experience personal?

Thinking of the pupil who did it, they were the class clown. To be honest, they probably would have spent the day going from lesson to lesson saying inappropriate things, and him seeing me in Asda presented him with an opportunity that was too good to miss. I don't think he knew me well enough at that stage to have harboured any feelings towards me.

3. How did the incident make you feel?

Like an idiot. Like I didn't know what I was doing, and also that I didn't know how to teach when I was wrong-footed as I went on to forget what topic I was delivering, creating a bit of a disaster. I then had to play catch-up in the next lesson to try and get them back on track.

4. Is there a repeat offender involved in the situation?

Yes! Classic class clown (ooh, the alliteration on that one!).

5. Were there any catalysts or red flags to the incident?

Honestly, no. It had been a pretty good lesson (or so I thought) up to that point and it came out of nowhere.

6. Have you decided to take any additional steps (e.g. call home, detention, involving another member of staff)?

No need, the head of department witnessed it so it stopped there and then.

7. Do you feel like leaving the classroom? Why?

Yes, because I don't know if I could deal with feeling humiliated like that regularly.

8. What's one thing that you would do differently if the same situation were to arise?

Move the conversation away more quickly. The moment I knew it was an off-task comment and he had his audience, I'd interrupt him and say we can talk about it at break if he wanted to discuss something outside of the topic.

So, now that we have started on our reflective journey together, with me leading by example, let me hand it over to you. Whatever made you pick up this book, whether it be gifted at the start of your teaching journey or sought out for some help along the way, let's start thinking, reflecting and most importantly smiling on the journey ahead.

Chapter 2

So... you lost control of the class today

There was once a pupil who had the ability to behave, but who would easily be distracted and loved to talk when the teacher was talking. In fact, this pupil was moved around the classroom so often that teachers would frequently give up on this method and move them to a different class altogether, but this wasn't a deterrent either, as they had the personality and social skills to talk to and distract *anyone* that they were sitting next to.

That pupil was me.

I sometimes believe that I am in teaching and have a keen interest in behaviour to readdress a karmic balance. In fact, I think this to be true of most teachers, especially those who liked to present their own challenges when they were at school.

I want to tell you the tale of a teacher we used to torture. At the time I didn't think we were that bad to them, but hindsight and QTS (qualified teacher status) give you a different point of view. This teacher really struggled to engage our class, a bright class who were all a little chopsy (probably one of the trickiest types of pupil: capable but they know it so don't try).

This teacher tried many tacks: bribery, sanctions, anger, bargaining, but by halfway through the year, she had clearly settled at a healthy balance of resentment and giving up. She would regularly threaten us with handing in her resignation because we were *that* awful (apparently). She even spent a lesson writing up said resignation, and when one of the smart-arses of my class pressed print and said we'd hand it in for her, her reaction made it very clear that she had no control of us, and the lunatics had just been given the keys to the asylum. I'm not proud of the actions that followed, including hiding under tables, going out of windows, sitting facing the back of the room when she was teaching at the front, and vice versa when she moved to the back to deliver (I don't think I should give a copy of this book to my parents...). It took our head of year to come in and threaten us with some pretty harsh outcomes (most of us were on sports teams and she was also a PE teacher so we were going to lose some 'representing the school' privileges) for us to wind our necks in and become half-decent human beings and a bit more respectful in her class.

I'm sure that member of staff is not looking back on our class with the fondness and mirth with which I look back on some of my crazy classes, but when I look back, I can think of all the ways that she lost control of our class, and never found a way to get us back onside. She lost us in Year 7, and if she came back across any of us in later years, I know things didn't generally go her way.

I'm sure almost every teacher has lost control of a class at some stage or another, no matter what their level of experience. If it's a one-off event, it's nothing to be ashamed of and no one is going to think any less of you. But you do need to put strategies in place to ensure it's not a regular occurrence or else you'll end up like my teacher all those years ago. To get us started with thinking about what we need to do here, let's look at it from an anonymous teacher's perspective.

Case study: Anonymous, experienced secondary teacher

I'm an experienced teacher, and a good part of my job is training and mentoring new teachers and colleagues in my school, which, by many measures, would be considered 'challenging'. Having taught the student body for a number of years now, however, with a clear strategy of quietly high expectations and consistently setting firm boundaries, I have few behavioural issues with my classes. In fact, many of the more problematic groups thrive under my raised eyebrow and unimpressed, soft-spoken persona.

In many ways, it's therefore embarrassing to share a story of a time when I lost complete control of my class so recently in my career. Yes, during my training and NQT year, I have some horror stories of locking doors against students trying to kick their way in, orange juice on my chair and computers toppled, and even one lesson that I've completely blocked out so traumatic was the experience, though I remember a bookshelf being involved at some point.

The class in question was a sweet Key Stage 3 class, who were actually being taught by my trainee teacher: a kind, gentle woman in her fifties, with a nurturing nature who enjoyed listening to the children's anecdotes in the middle of a lesson, while the rest of the class patiently highlighted their books or threw bits of paper at each other. Her approach, however, was exactly what was needed for the many students in the class on the autistic spectrum who thrived on her quiet attention as they rattled on about cacti.

When my trainee was off sick for two days, I stepped in to take over the reins and many of the students quickly surmised that this stern lady – who had until that point sat in various chairs in the classroom and reprimanded them with all the warmth of a marble statue – would neither allow a lengthy narrative about kittens, nor be impressed by a date and title without starter notes, regardless of how neatly said date and title were underlined.

Obviously, such an approach did not work for one of our autistic students. The change of teacher, combined with a tiring day, a long term and explosive incidents in other lessons over the last few weeks with peers in the same class, was a recipe for eruption.

In short: he made strange noises, another of our ASD (autism spectrum disorder) students got cross, I gave them both a warning and the situation escalated from there until the first student was shouting and screaming at the entire class that he would kill them if they laughed at him or said anything to him again. It was genuinely like something from one of my worst nightmares, the scene made poignantly worse by a third ASD student who sat next to the first and could only stare down at his desk, hunched over like a tortoise, protecting himself from the sensory overload.

I emailed for support, and the situation continued to escalate – the upset young man being incredibly articulate in his death threats, the teenage girls in the class tittering and sniggering awkwardly at the outburst, and the second student protesting the injustice of the insults.

Support came quickly: in fact, I heard the SENCO (special educational needs coordinator), inclusion officer and two members of the SLT actually running down the corridor, so known was the student for his episodes. They intervened gently but firmly, but this young man would not budge, becoming (understandably) more and more upset by the whole situation.

After what must have only been a few minutes, but which felt like my entire career frozen in horror in front of me, the SENCO made the decision to move not the student in question but the entire class to a room downstairs. Now, this was a sensible idea, and one that I am sure the SENCO considers one of a number of tools in her belt of de-escalating strategies, but in 11 years, I had never had an entire class filed out of my room, row by row, by four senior members of staff to walk silently down the stairs to a colleague's classroom because I, as an experienced and respected teacher, had misjudged a situation.

While the SENCO and inclusion officer took the time to comfort and reassure me at the end of the day, the incident marked me with a sense of shame and failure, partly because I felt that there must have been something that I could have done to avoid such a scenario, but also because the system that we were working in was stretching this child so thin that he had no other way to express himself than to shout, scream, threaten and yell.

Tips I took away? Before and after this lesson, I have spent time with this child: he thrives on one-to-one connection, on talking about funny little things he notices around him – he offers beautiful and considerate insights on texts and characters. But he has no statement, no funding attached to him for the TA that he needs, nor sufficient knowledge or financial resources at home to gain access to a school that will support his needs.

While our anonymous contributor's story is very different to my own, they both show the importance of understanding and recognising the needs of individual students. The mindset I had as an easily distracted pupil has always given me a bit of an edge when dealing with behaviour situations for myself. Putting yourself in the position of the pupil gives you the option and time for you to be able to step back and develop a plan of action, whilst also walking in their shoes, because we were all that age once.

It is always a trickier scenario when we are thinking about a class that has been disrupted by one of our children who is on the SEN register. It doesn't make it any less difficult, but we have to think of ways to work in our inclusive classrooms without suffering too much lost learning. As a

SENCO, I have always led with the importance of quality-first teaching, but there is also the need to understand and recognise the needs of the individual. Whether they have social, emotional and mental health (SEMH) needs or are placed on the autistic spectrum, display signs of global learning delay or in fact have any additional needs that will be a factor in contributing towards adverse behaviour, it is important that you take the time to get a real understanding of that pupil. This may be through reading and understanding their support plan, liaising with the SENCO or inclusion lead for further tips on how to work with them, or even talking to the child themselves. Never underestimate the monumental power of student voice.

With these great stories in mind, what could we do to regain control of a class that is spiralling out of control – and prevent it from happening again in the future?

Classroom management

When we think of losing control of our classrooms, we first have to address our techniques of classroom management. But what does this commonly used term actually mean and what does 'good classroom management' involve?

Back in 1999, Carolyn Evertson and Alene Harris argued that classroom management mustn't focus purely on disciplinary practices and behavioural interventions and should instead move towards a more holistic definition that involves teachers developing a supportive learning environment. Brophy (1999) believes that classroom management is a process and classroom management can be defined as a particular capacity for having an effective learning environment, which is managed by the most successful teachers. Erden (2008) defines classroom management as a process including various kinds of techniques and activities in order to create an effective learning environment and maintain effective student behaviours in parallel to the objectives of the teaching and learning process. Borko and Putnam (1995) believe that teaching strategies are part of the classroom management skills needed by a teacher in order to set up rules and procedures of the classroom, to organise learning groups, to monitor learning of the students and events affecting the learning of the students, to arrange the possible learning pace and to manage misbehaviour that may arise.

So, from the research we know that classroom management shouldn't just be about reacting to behavioural incidents as and when they arise via interventions or sanctions. You have to be proactive in setting rules and routines that prevent disruptive behaviour in the first place. But what does this actually look like in practice? Well, you need to find time to provide behaviour-learning opportunities alongside your curriculum.

Behaviour-learning opportunities

Looking at the curriculum that you will be delivering, and seeing where there might be time and space to provide behaviour-learning opportunities, could be the difference to your being able to fire through the curriculum for the rest of the year with minimal behaviour interventions with a tricky class, and your constantly being at a loss for how to make progress when it's clear learning is not happening due to all of the distractions.

If you can put in the groundwork initially in the first few lessons, you will leave yourself only having to build in refresher sessions (more on those on page 34) throughout the rest of the year and ultimately maintaining a strong presence based on cues and routines. This works no matter what age group you are teaching: I don't see an age range being imposed on this principle, only a need for adapting the plays in your playbook.

There are some topics that lend themselves well to setting out your rules and routines. As an ICT teacher, I could find creativity in a lesson revolving around how programming commands work when writing a program. The premise of the lesson would be to include commands that could be acted out in the lesson. For example, I would tell them that when the light is switched off they were allowed to talk, but whenever the light was on they needed to stop straight away:

'If light on volume up, if light off volume down.'

I could even introduce an else function:

'Else, 2 minutes at breaktime.'

While this is more of a Key Stage 3 approach, if you take some time to think about your medium-term plan for the year, you will see areas and topics in your phase and subject area where these learning opportunities will jump out. A note in your teacher planner can be enough to provide you with the direction you want to take in these lessons.

But what about when the class is already out of control and you're tearing your hair out over what to do to get them to settle again? Here are some of my best plays that you can add to your playbook to try out next time you find yourself faced with this situation.

Plays for the playbook

Resetter

When the class has lost all its ability to focus, and chaos is tapping at the door, I like to use this as a way of resetting their brains whilst simultaneously expending some of the energy that has no doubt led them to this point. I particularly like to use this in the summer after they have come in from a lunchtime feeling hyped up and distracted.

In pairs, get them to stand facing each other and pick someone to come to the front of the room to demonstrate. I tend to pick the pupil most likely to cause destruction and distraction so that they can take ownership, but also so they can be involved in positive interaction in the lesson. Now move through these steps:

Step 1

Tell the class that they are going to count to three with their partner, but they are going to alternate the numbers between them. Face your pupil and count one, point to them for them to say two, and then point back at yourself to say three. Point at them to say one, point at yourself to say two, and point at them to say three. Now say one without pointing and hopefully your pupil will have picked it up by now.

Step 2

Cycle through a few times before asking the class to have a go. Let them do it for about 20 seconds.

Step 3

Explain to them that you're now going to start introducing some changes and the numbers are going to start disappearing. Instead of saying one, you're now going to click your fingers. Demonstrate:

You: Click.

Pupil: Two.

You: Three.

Pupil: Click.

You: Two.

Pupil: Three.

Get the class to have a go.

Step 4

The number two is going to start disappearing now and being replaced with a clap.

Step 5

There are no more numbers from this point on, as you're going to stamp your feet for three.

By this point, the class should be quiet, other than concentrating on getting the click, clap and stamp. This new noise level enables you to get them to sit quietly. Thank them for participating and remind them that we want to remain focused on the learning task at hand now.

Pattern interrupts

A pattern interrupt can be a useful technique for breaking a recurring cycle of disruptive behaviour. The technique is used with Neuro Linguistic Programming (NLP) and is considered a series of interruptions that break a habit or a state. There are lots of quick and easy strategies you can use as pattern interrupters to stop one pupil or a whole class of pupils from engaging in an unwanted behaviour and get the learning back on track for everyone. As you'll see, some of these strategies are instantaneous and will take only a few seconds to implement, but others are a bit longer. You should aim for them to last a maximum of four minutes:

Time to explain – 1 minute

Time to execute – 3 minutes

Total time to resettle – 4 minutes

I'm going to give you some examples that can be thrown into your playbook, but go away and research some more options, experiment with what would work for you, and which areas are more suited to which key stage, which subject, which time of the day and which season of the year. Surprisingly (or unsurprisingly), these are all factors that need to play into your decisions to make the right call. The following are examples of ideas that I would use in EYFS and Key Stages 1, 2 and 3.

Call and response

A timeless classic: you call out a phrase and your class calls out a response. I've selected some of my favourites here for you to try. A lot may feel quite American because they're a big fan of using these on their summer camps. Having been a camp manager for a summer camp myself, I can tell you the effectiveness of these is unrivalled. If you can get 200 to 800 campers refocused and listening to instructions when there is a melee of excitement and a buzz of activity, usually in a hall with terrible acoustics and an untold number of distractions, then you're onto a winner with a class of 30.

> *Ready, set... You bet.*
> *Hocus pocus... Time to focus.*
> *Holy moly... Guacamole.*
> *Hands on top... Everybody stop.*
> *Zip zip zap... We're all that.*
> *To infinity... And beyond.*
> *Can I get a ... Whoop whoop.*
> *Stop... Collaborate and listen.*
> *Macaroni and cheese... Everybody freeze.*

Tootsie Roll, lollipop… We've been talking, now let's stop.
L-I-S… T-E-N.
All set?… You bet.
Ready to rock… Ready to roll.
Shark bait… Oohh ha ha. (Think Finding Nemo.*)*
Scooby Dooby Doo… Where are you?
Flat tyre… Shhhhhh.
One two three, eyes on me… One two, eyes on you. (The classic.)
If you can hear me, put your hands on your knees.

I hope you have as much fun using these as I did typing them. The smile and endorphins I get from hearing them in my head are unrivalled to when you are teaching in March and you can get back the attention of the class so easily with a smile plastered across your face!

Training is key to making this play work. Ask pupils to come up with their own at the start of your time teaching them. This is a great lesson alongside establishing class rules. Turn it into a group-work activity, with a vote and a competition. No matter the subject, it allows for some rapport-building from the outset. It also allows ownership and investment in the system as well, so if they are not following it, you have an added motivation to get them back on board.

The 'Give Me Five' technique

Harry and Rosemary Wong, authors of *The First Days of School: How to be an effective teacher* (2018), coined this technique. The teacher raises his or her hands and the class follows. As each finger is lifted, everyone says:

1. eyes – look
2. ears – listen
3. mouth – closed
4. hands – still
5. feet – quiet.

Your class should be quiet in five seconds.

Visualise noise

There are apps out there which you can put on the board that will allow pupils themselves to be in charge of the noise levels in the classroom because they can see very clearly where it is at. Explain to them the level that they are allowed to go to for the task. Different tasks can be assigned different levels at the start of the year. An individual task, teacher talk or class presentations may require silence; paired work may be slightly higher and group work even higher. The different levels can be colour-coded and shown in displays around your room. For example:

> 'This task is a Blue noise level activity, so while you may be having a conversation with the person sitting next to you, I shouldn't be able to hear what you're saying.'

A clap routine

Clap your hands and in a normal tone of voice say, 'Clap once if you can hear me.' Those students who hear you will clap. Then say, 'Clap twice if you can hear me.' More kids respond with two claps. Go on to three, four, five... By this time, you should have the attention of your students.

'Simon says'

The teacher says, 'touch your nose', 'pat your head' or 'point to the teacher'. Instructing students to use their hands gets them to drop the objects they are holding and focus.

Exercise break

This is similar to the resetter (see page 27), but for this one you're asking them to get up and quickly expel some energy. You can get them out of their chairs and try some jumping jacks, running on the spot or sit-ups. I have even been known to take the class on a quick lap outside, but only if I know I can trust them not to disturb the lessons around them when moving through the school. The learning time lost is minimal and sometimes needed, especially if time of day or weather play a factor in how unsettled your class are. When you get back, you can play it like you've done them a favour by getting out for a few minutes. This tactic is a rarity and to be used incredibly sparingly so that they don't continue to think that chaos gets them out of work. You must explain that twice as much work and focus needs to be in place on their return.

Whisper instructions

(Especially strange instructions.) The kids in the front will start to follow and the others will try and figure out what you're saying and what their classmates are doing.

Target word

Ask the students to pick a word that's related to what they're studying. Some examples include 'dinosaur', 'adjective' or 'New York'. When you say the word, the children should stop and wait for directions. Or, the children could respond with a definition or short response to the target word, for example, if you said, 'New York', the students would respond, 'The Big Apple!'

Strategies for Key Stages 4 and 5

While I would say that any of the above techniques may best be geared towards a younger audience, never underestimate the nostalgia and engagement that pupils in Key Stages 4 and 5 may show when using them too. However, here are also some bespoke suggestions for our older counterparts.

Employ a mini teacher

Ask a pupil to come to the front. I sometimes pick someone who has been instrumental in the noise and disruption. I introduce them by their surname and let the class know that 'Ms Johnson will be taking the class for the next five minutes, so please give her the respect and attention she deserves.' This change of tack is enough to get them interested in what is going on. Hand over your spot and sit where the mini teacher was sitting. Depending on their mood, you can be a helpful student to them or an annoying one. Allow them to deliver for a bit, and once the class has refocused, thank them and take back over and continue the lesson.

Voting

Ask a question related to the lesson and get your students to vote as the response. There are many apps that can let the class interact with the question. An interruption to the session to bring an interactive activity can help with reengagement and refocusing.

Deliberate mistakes

Announce that you intend to make deliberate errors on the board, on a handout or in your speech, and ask your students to catch you if they can. (You can be funny or add in random facts like, 'Did you know that it was actually Mrs C-S who passed the Education Act of 1982?')

Powerful images

Hold up or display an image of something related to your lessons without any context, as an attention-grabber, such as a chemical reaction, a history scene or a graph with two geometric shapes. Ask the students to write a caption.

Countdown conundrum

Write a scrambled word (related to your lesson) on the board, for example, 'het nureltovoi' (The Revolution), and ask students to unscramble it.

Hangman

Play a round of hangman with a keyword from the topic.

Quotation time

Display two quotations that don't seem to be related to one another and ask – not just how they are related to each other – but how they are related to the day's lesson as well.

Humanise yourself

Never underestimate the power of 'Did you see *Love Island* last night?' Facilitate a quick discussion, then use this new focus to flip back to the task: 'Talking of how Samira got voted out, let's talk about some chemical reactions that occur when certain elements are removed.'

Refresher lessons

As with everything, complacency can be the enemy of progress. As the year goes on, and you hit your stride and your class gets comfortable with you and your expectations, I find that it works well to punctuate a term with a reminder of some of these playbook plays. You may do this automatically without thinking, and usually a time when this happens is at the start of each term. It can be done as simply as putting a slide up reminding pupils of your classroom expectations, the school's expectations and the rules and routines of your classroom.

Reflective space: So... you lost control of the class today

We've spoken about being reflective practitioners on this journey, so here's your space to get those thoughts down. Think of a scenario that you have been in with an unsettled class, and the way in which you could have analysed it at the time. Apply some of these questions, and any more of your own, and get your reflective juices flowing.

1. What happened?

_____

_____

_____

_____

2. Was this experience personal?

_____

_____

_____

_____

3. How did the incident make you feel?

_____

_____

_____

_____

4. Is there a repeat offender involved in the situation?

_____

_____

_____

_____

5. Were there any catalysts or red flags to the incident?

_____

_____

_____

_____

6. Have you decided to take any additional steps (e.g. call home, detention, involving another member of staff)?

_____

_____

_____

_____

7. Do you feel like leaving the classroom? Why?

_____

_____

_____

_____

8. What's one thing that you would do differently if the same situation were to arise?

_____

_____

_____

_____

Chapter 3

So... you embarrassed yourself in front of your pupils

I didn't have to dig too deep into the archives for anecdotes for this chapter. My biggest problem was trying to pick *one* incident, because one thing that you'll discover (or know) as a teacher is that there is a plethora of opportunities to embarrass yourself, and the beauty of working with children is that they have absolutely zero problem in not only pointing it out (loudly), but also igniting the torch paper to somehow let the entire school know before you have even left the scene of the crime. I definitely could have filled this chapter with slapstick befitting of a post-war BBC comedy. The anecdote I am going to share may lose the fellas in the room, but this is something that I think might be a good bit of advice for any teacher and may help give birth to the 'Make sure you can't see up it, down it or through it' self-imposed rule when it comes to choosing the outfit that you are going to wear to school.

I don't know how to say that I have an ample bosom without sounding like an old school ma'am. So, I'm just going to say that I have a large chest, and let me tell you about the first and last day that I wore a button-down shirt to school without a vest top underneath. I was an NQT (the year I think all of my biggest mistakes happened) and was very proud of my latest clothes haul for my new job, especially as most of them had come off the reduced clothes rack. A few frayed threads here, a few loose buttons there. All things that were worth mending for the 20 per cent off. Except, of course, I never got round to mending anything.

As an ICT teacher, you can spend a large proportion of your lesson bending over a computer to help and support. I don't know if it was the strain of my chest, the wind, or a child praying for a distraction so that I wouldn't ask for the homework they hadn't done, but the single button that had been keeping my modesty under wraps had decided that the Year 9 class after lunch with the most poorly behaved boys in the year group was the time to make its bid for freedom.

I'm going to leave most of this to your imagination in the interest of preserving my status as a DSL, but what then happened can only be related to when someone drops a glass in a pub. This was a situation that none of my class were equipped with the emotional capacity or maturity to deal with, and to be honest, I don't think I was either.

So how did I handle it? I decided to pretend like nothing had happened, even with the hysteria of 'Miss, that hit me in my eye! I'm suing.' I laughed, walked out of the classroom and asked my head of department to look after my class whilst I sprinted to the technology block to beg the textiles teacher for a safety pin. If you ever come to my office these days, check my drawer and you'll always find at least eight safety pins and a sewing kit!

Luckily, I'm not the only one who has found themselves in embarrassing situations, as Sophie and Rosie will let you see in these case studies.

Case study: Sophie Beamish, secondary English teacher

As an eager new teacher, I had all the idealistic optimism everybody does: I was going to inspire, innovate and create change. My students would drink up every word I said. I definitely make a difference; I think I can be inspiring and innovative but nothing had prepared me for one of my first classes. It was a Year 10 class, one of the lowest sets possible, who had been condemned to supply teachers for the previous two years. They had huge gaps in their knowledge, were a mixed bag of needs (EAL, SEN, low-ability, behavioural) and, as I was informed on my very first day as an untrained, inexperienced teacher, they would be taking their GCSE English language exam a year early.

The class quickly became my biggest challenge and making it through a 'Do Now' and 'Starter' task in the course of a 60-minute lesson was an achievement. Many of the popular students were in my class, as well as diligent, but sadly low-attaining, students. The diligent students really wanted to achieve; the popular students were concerned with their social lives, chaotic home situations and their 'street cred'. As such, my 'class cred' became incredibly important. I was in a war to make these students care and realise their potential, and any weakness on my part would mean certain failure. As well as adopting a 'firm but fair' demeanour to counteract the weakness they seemed to see in my relative youth (I was very obviously a 21-year-old new teacher), I began wearing boots with chunky heels in an attempt to 'assert my authority' with my Year 10 students since many of the boys (and girls) were taller than me or at least my height. In the midst of another lesson (battle) with Year 10, I had managed to engage the class. They were actually listening, contributing, writing! OK, we were still on the starter and it was a relatively short and accessible task but still... victory. I felt triumphant, inspiring and innovative – all the things I'd dreamt I'd be. My euphoria was short-lived; it seemed fate, and my trusty boots, had other ideas.

I was at the front of the class, leading the discussion as students fed back their ideas, and trying my best to keep everyone focused and on track – I was desperate for the students to continue contributing and to hold onto one of the rare teaching episodes I had managed to gain with this class. Every eye was on me, the class was quiet, they were listening to a contribution, a couple of the more diligent students had their hands up, the challenging students were quiet. I was barely containing my joy and I began to question the student who had contributed and then... my heel snapped. It broke. Leg to jelly, ankle and foot caved in on themselves and I crashed to the floor. No decorum, no dignity. Shock came over the classroom, concern on the diligent students' faces, glee on the more challenging students' faces.

Horror.

I'd well and truly lost the battle and I'd never regain any dignity or opportunity to teach for the next two years. So, I did the only thing I could do. I laughed. It was funny. What else could I do? I pulled myself up and laughed. Not fake laughter but genuine.

Embarrassing yourself in front of a class, particularly a difficult class, feels horrific in the moment. But laughing along with them was the best thing I could have done. The students got to see behind the teacher façade to the clumsy human being whom many an incident of this ilk had befallen. You need to let students see this side of you in order to form relationships. Attempting to sanction or tell them off is pointless – whatever you said or did *was* embarrassing and therefore, to your students, comical.

Once the laughter subsides, however, it is important to regain control. The classroom is your space, the lesson is yours and they are your class, so take ownership of the embarrassing incident. You allowed them the joke but now it's time to move on and if they can't, then sanctions will be given. My 'ownership' came in the form of taking off the broken boots and teaching in my socks. I made it clear that we (emphasis on the 'we') had had a laugh but it was time to move on. I continued my questioning; the class followed suit and the incident bizarrely seemed to help rather than hinder our relationship. It became something we reminisced and laughed about together rather than something they used against me and, while they remained my most difficult class, they became my most rewarding class precisely because of the effort I had to put into forming relationships with them.

Sophie Beamish has been teaching for four years and is currently a teacher of English and on the whole-school literacy team. It has been two years since she completed her NQT year.

We have all been there at the moment of a wardrobe malfunction, but to do it in the presence of 14- and 15-year-olds is likely to take it to the next level of embarrassment. I'm here for you, Sophie. Please join us at Bad Clothes Day Anonymous whenever you're ready. We have a new pair of boots waiting for you!

Rosie Birks, English and maths teacher

Crying, bleeding and clutching a jar of mayonnaise to my swollen knee was embarrassing. I still cringe when I remember 30 13-year-olds staring at me with shock and sympathy.

On the way to my library lesson, I had tripped over a drain cover, dislocated my knee, and shredded my tights and skin alike. I had, however, magically managed to save the cup of tea I was carrying.

This was all in front of herds of students as they left the refectory after devouring their breaktime snacks. I do not remember if the kids laughed. I would not have blamed them if they did. I did. Shock must have kicked in, as I wobbled to my feet, forcing a smile through gritted teeth. I asked some kids to fetch some crutches from medical and limped to the library lesson, just as the blood from my grazed leg started to peep through the black holes.

'You're late,' the librarian snarled as I hobbled through the door.

That was it. My lips started to tremble, my eyes filled with water and my knee throbbed. My class were rightly confused, but they rallied. They pulled two chairs up and went to fetch some ice. Instead, they returned with a jar of mayonnaise. I told them all I was fine. It happens all the time; I just needed a sit down. I did not admit that the tears would not stop because I was mortified and hurting. This only prolonged my embarrassment. I felt weak and useless. It was a very long lesson.

I was on crutches for a couple of weeks afterwards and forced myself into school. I did lose a few hours of sleep, generating all the insults and quips my class were going to make about me, to me. Everyone knew classes could smell weakness and fear, right? They were going to destroy me.

But they did not. They were kind and considerate and once they'd checked I was OK and that I wasn't going to cry again, slowly we began to smile about it.

That was four years ago now.

'Remember when you fell over?' still surfaces a few times a year, as if I could ever forget it. My stomach does not tighten as much when I recall the incident now. The students taught me that everyone falls over and I taught them that everyone cries.

I have cried in front of classes since (when Auggie Pullman's dog died in *Wonder* just after we lost our own family dog, that triggered the waterworks) and I will probably cry in front of classes in the future. My mum cries at adverts and *Deal or No Deal*, but it has taken me a while to get used to also being a blubberer.

But that is not my advice for you, although I think it is important to ensure we are portrayed as real human beings with real human emotions. My message, to save you from the humiliation I suffered, is to ask for help when you need it. It is OK to say you have made a mistake or had an accident, and your colleagues are there to support and save you.

Since my fall, a colleague has knocked into me in the staff room. I was pouring a fresh cup of boiling black coffee, which really complimented my white shirt as it scolded my chest. I went straight to medical, where the textiles teacher found me a clean top, the food tech teacher clingfilmed my scolded skin, and off I was sent to the pharmacy for burns cream and a cold shower. In October last year, I chipped the bottom off my ankle bone playing badminton with colleagues. Subsequently, I tried to stand up on my own. Apparently, I went very pale just as the room started spinning and I almost passed out. I allowed myself to be bundled into a wheelchair and taken to A&E with a bag of ice. The only thing I was embarrassed about this time was that I had not painted my toenails in a while.

In hindsight, I could have looked where I was walking on my way to that library lesson. I could have gone straight to the medical room and asked the nurse to look at it. I could have gone to the nearest office and asked for help. But I did not do any of those things. Idiot. I did not want to admit that I was hurt or clumsy, and wanted to save face. I did not want to ask for help because I was embarrassed, and that led to even more embarrassment. Sometimes it takes more strength to ask for help than struggling on alone.

Rosie Birks is a head of house and a teacher of English and mathematics. She's been teaching for five years since her NQT year.

You've got to love a series of stories that make you simultaneously cringe and also feel relief that it wasn't you... until you remember a situation where something like this *did* in fact happen to you. Ah the shame spiral. That's OK though, because we can use the rest of the chapter to reflect on it and get a plan ready for next time (because there will be a next time, and it'll be when you least expect it!).

Plays for the playbook

Own the situation

Ignoring the situation may not work in your favour. It could lead to the class not being able to move on from the situation. Facing it head on can allow you to take ownership of the situation, but it also allows you to put 'a full stop and now it's time to move on' narrative to the class.

Think about what type of teacher you are in the face of embarrassment

Are you likely to want the ground to swallow you up so you can disappear? Are you able to think on your feet and make a quick quip about it? Are you a crier? Considering in advance how you might be likely to react to an embarrassing situation will prepare you for dealing with it when one does come along. Things are going to go wrong, hopefully not all the time, but all you can do is try to prepare. At a recent speaking function where I myself fell over because my heel suddenly snapped, I realised I'm not fully sure how much you can prepare for every eventuality, and the more experienced you are doesn't necessarily reduce the chances of embarrassment. But if you at least know how you're going to react to a situation, your tears or your quick wit won't take you by surprise. Having a set of retorts in your brain will help you change the direction of the attention as well as show that you have control of the situation: it's not a big deal, so let's move on. If you take the fuel away from the flame, the fire can't be fanned, and it will go out much more quickly than you'd think it could.

Embrace the emotions felt by the class

Let's be honest, in some of these situations, the pupils are going to be just as embarrassed as you are. Try not to shoot them down too much, but offer an alternative time to discuss it so that they continue with their learning. I'm sure they may continue to discuss it at lunchtime, but it's highly unlikely they're going to want to talk with you about it... but at least the option is there!

Tell a colleague

I would recommend the first time you discuss a hugely embarrassing situation it isn't in a published book. I wish at the time that I had gone to the staff room and shared my button-popping-off incident, because I have no doubt that my colleagues would have laughed with me. Most definitely they would have taken the mick out of me mercilessly, but then they would have been supportive and no doubt shared their own woes, which would have made me feel a whole lot better. There is an illusion that teachers are meant to be perfect. We are role models after all, but I will always come back to the concept that we are but mortals.

Remember, it's in the past

It's happened, you can't change it. It can be so easy to revisit and relive the experience time and time again. Even if you have those moments where you remember suddenly and it hits you like a gut punch, or you wake in the middle of the night after reliving it in a dream, or worse, you're wide awake thinking about it at 4 am, figuring how you could have lived the moment so differently. Just remember, it's been and gone. That moment cannot come back unless you let it haunt you. It's nice to remember that all embarrassment takes place in the past!

Stop apologising

A thoroughly British trait is to continually apologise for those moments that leave us puce. But continually apologising puts us back in the scenario of reliving a moment that really should be left behind.

Get perspective

In the scheme of things, how bad was the experience? Like really? How bad? Because if you are in a situation of embarrassment while being a teacher, I can almost guarantee that it is not a scenario that you have entered into willingly. We end up in situations where, although you'd rather not be there, the ever-immortal words of Mr Chow in *The Hangover*, 'But did you die?!', always ring true for getting a little perspective on the event.

Get back on the horse

There is no point in trying to get that hole in the ground to appear and have it swallow you up forever. You can't avoid the situation forever and you can't stay away from the scene of the crime! The best thing to do is to get back on the horse and create new, more positive experiences in the same place so that you can override the automatic shame cycle you could step into when you are in the same location in future.

Untangle what you are feeling

Is the situation you are in enough to make you experience shame? If so, why? Unpack those emotions by finding a sounding board to talk to and unload and evaluate those emotions, whether that is in a supervision session, talking to your line manager or a debrief with a friend over a cocktail or a pint.

Overcome the physiological overtones

Unclench, take a deep breath, count to ten, relax your shoulders, shake it off. Find what works for you to reduce your adrenaline in the moment so that you can move forward as quickly as you can.

Live, learn and laugh it off

I think you already know from the title that the aim of this book is to get you to a position where you can laugh off some of our most mortifying teaching experiences. Achieving water off a duck's back mode is what we are aiming for, so flex those facial muscles, get those teeth on show and get a plan of action not to be in the position to live it again!

> ## Reflective space: So... you embarrassed yourself in front of your pupils

Think back to a moment when you felt mortified in front of a class. Your instinct at the time might have been to brush it under the carpet and pretend it never happened. But that's not going to help you in the long run. So, be brave and unpick what happened in that moment and its aftermath, and think carefully about how you'll react next time you find yourself in a similar situation. Write down some notes in response to the following questions to help you.

1. What happened?

_____

_____

_____

_____

2. Was this experience personal?

_____

_____

_____

_____

3. How did the incident make you feel?

_____

_____

_____

_____

4. Is there a repeat offender involved in the situation?

_____

_____

_____

_____

5. Were there any catalysts or red flags to the incident?

_____

_____

_____

_____

6. Have you decided to take any additional steps (e.g. call home, detention, involving another member of staff)?

_____

_____

_____

_____

7. Do you feel like leaving the classroom? Why?

_____

_____

_____

_____

8. What's one thing that you would do differently if the same situation were to arise?

_____

_____

_____

_____

Chapter 4

So... that kid outsmarted you, huh?

Not possible. We are the adults; therefore we are in charge and in control at all times. Also, we have so much world experience that there is no chance that someone who has been on the earth for considerably less time than us could possibly get one up on us.

Let go of that notion straight away. Never underestimate the potential of some of the evil geniuses that we teach. And I say that fondly, as some of these characters are the pupils who make me laugh and I love being a part of moulding the next generation.

When I was in my training year, I had a very tricky placement. That's how it was sold to us: no smoke and mirrors, just a black and white scenario and brace yourself for the ride. Now that I look back, it was definitely livelier than most schools, but I'm incredibly grateful that it was one of my foundation blocks to teaching, even if it felt like its main service was to keep me on my toes. Thinking back to a Level 1 ICT lesson, I realised that this was a group of pupils who unfortunately had not got their first-choice options (for varying reasons, some I agreed with, most I disagreed with), so were placed into this lesson. Meaning that they had no passion for the topic and were happy to do less than the bare minimum.

This meant that I started to do everything that I could to try and engage them with the topic. You name it, I probably did it to try and keep them learning and attending my lessons. Anything that may have worked one week (e.g. stickers) didn't seem to have any traction the next lesson. That was until I came across using music. It became a way to focus them and acted as a reward system. It also became punitive, which they took great umbrage to. I had made a rod for my own back. In most other lessons they weren't allowed the radio on, but I decided that there was a loophole, as it *was* allowed in art and design technology because it was a creative faculty. I thought that as ICT lay within this same faculty at this school, it would be OK for me to do the same.

One week, after a pretty dreadful previous lesson, I had decided that they wouldn't have the music on that day. They were not happy with this decision and decided that throughout the duration of the lesson they would try to listen to music from their phones with their own personal headphones. Feeling smug as I confiscated the earphones one by one, I decided to (foolishly) exclaim, 'You guys aren't even clever with it. When I was at school, we used to thread the cable up through our blazers, down the sleeves and then lean in on our hands as if we were listening intently, but really be listening to the radio.'

Next lesson I thought I'd nailed my behaviour management of the class, that they were all engaged, doting on my every word. Their postures had changed from swinging on chairs to facing forward leaning on their hands, almost looking at me adoringly. It took me a good 15 minutes and walking past a boy with Eminem blaring tinnily out of his blazer for me to put two and two together and get my first 'outsmarted teacher' accolade. Dammit!

Luckily, I'm not the only one who has received this wonderful piece of silverware during their teaching tenure as Zanna and a mystery contributor can tell you now.

Case study: Zanna, EYFS teacher

You'd think in the EYFS (Early Years Foundation Stage) it's pretty easy to stay one step ahead of the four-year-olds in your class, and they are certainly more interested in stickers or high-fives than secondary students would be. But they are also less used to following behaviour expectations, and they don't have the appropriateness filter that an older child might have.

By the spring term in reception, most children are able to write phrases or captions with minimal support, and in the spring of my NQT year, we were lucky enough to have chicks to write about. Most of the class took to the task with enthusiasm, but one child was not in the mood. After she scribbled over the lines of her first sheet, I told her she must not leave the table until she'd written a proper sentence. A few minutes later, she approached me with a smirk on her face, brandishing her second sheet.

'I've written a sentence,' she told me gleefully. And so she had. Complete with a capital letter, finger spaces and a full stop, she had written:

'I think Miss [my name] hates me.'

I felt awful and started apologising and reassuring her, and that smile of victory just got bigger and bigger. She had totally manipulated me and she knew it.

How did I handle it? When I realised I'd been played by this usually puppy-eyed four-year-old, I said maybe it would be best, then, if she wrote about the chicks in another classroom. She did so, and came back with a very sweet apology. She assured me that she knew we were friends really. We usually get on very well, but I still think she knows my secret – that I value positive relationships with my students a great deal – and I wouldn't put it past her to attempt to use that to her advantage again.

On the plus side, her independent sentence is a great example of her having met expected standard in writing, but I'd be cautious to present it for moderation! And while some children might exploit it occasionally, letting my class know that I care about them has always proved successful in the end.

My tip for you is that I'd say that being genuine and honest, while maintaining appropriate boundaries, is really beneficial. Children work best when they know that they can trust you. I also think that you find out what children are capable of in unusual situations – it was the first time this child had written an independent sentence, so although she kind of beat me, I also found out what she was able to do. If a child is smart enough to have a witty comeback, they're smart enough to achieve great things in their learning, and it can help to tell them that you know that!

Zanna is an EYFS teacher who has been practising for one year since being an NQT.

Oh, we all love that moment when we realise we've been played by someone who is years our junior. Take some solace, Zanna, in the idea that there are more in the club than would probably care to admit to it. Cue our next anonymous contributor. I did not challenge their right to anonymity. Instead I read the story, had a belly laugh and went forward to put in measures to protect their identity. If you could all read this in an actor's voice, it would be greatly appreciated.

Case study: Anonymous, secondary maths teacher

When I got to my first placement school I was given a middle-set maths class. They were a lovely group and generally well behaved, but I had a class clown who, whenever he became stuck on work, would begin to play up. Let's call the pupil Tom. Tom was not doing so well in my maths lesson, but had a mum who was very keen that he would, so I found that if I wrote a note in his homework diary about his work ethic or behaviour, his mum would respond, often by telling me what item he had lost as a consequence.

Towards the end of my placement, I realised that my final placement was going to take place at the same school and I was going to keep the same classes, so Tom, as an issue to my teaching and learning, was not going to go away.

I spent the last few lessons implementing all the tools that I could think of to try and get him engaged and think about turning over a new leaf. Nothing worked.

Cut to returning for my final placement. I faced his lesson with some trepidation and anxiety, but again got myself ready with all my fresh teacher training skills. As I took out my laminated resources ready to keep him on task and focused, I asked the class some questions, and Tom was the first one with his hand up, answering every question. I didn't know what had happened, but he was a new pupil. He was able to work out any maths in a second. He had me convinced that the work I had put in had turned him into a human calculator. The speed with which he could complete the questions proved this. He was so quick at answering that sometimes, if you didn't know better, it was almost as if he was answering the questions before I had even asked them. He was in one of my Year 9 maths classes, a class that was shared by myself and another member of staff. I taught a few Year 9 classes, and had got into a nice momentum of sharing the lesson plans across the groups, as they were all at a similar learning capacity.

Lessons were going by and Tom was really flying at a rate that I hadn't seen before. The previous data that I had been given for him was showing a rapid sense of improvement. I was feeling quite smug and even boasted about it in the staff room, loud enough for his head of year to comment how very out of character this was for Tom, and would I mind if he came and observed the next lesson? Obviously I said yes, feeling a sense of inflated pride.

When the head of year turned up, the pupils were a lot quieter than usual, and Tom seemed to start squirming in his chair when I called on him for a question. The head of year thanked me and asked Tom to come and see him at break. It was then that the colour drained from Tom's face.

It turns out that Tom wasn't Tom at all, and Tom was in fact Reece. They were twins who had jumped on the opportunity to get Tom's maths grades up as there was a temporary teacher in the room who was never going to figure it out: me. Their plan had only been able to be carried out because Reece's teacher was on long-term sick leave.

I'd been outsmarted by a set of twins, which was only made harder by the fact that I didn't even know they were outsmarting me!

Advice? No matter how long you have been in a school, if you have the ability to see a set of class photos, look at them carefully and learn the distinguishing features of all the students in your class!

What I love about these anecdotes is the fact that it doesn't matter the age or even how many pupils are (knowingly or unknowingly) involved, being outsmarted can come in many guises, whether it is having your knowledge used against you, or being in a lesson and realising that they know more on the topic than you. This can happen. And that's OK. Try adding these plays to your playbook to get one step ahead next time.

Plays for the playbook

What if they know more on the topic?

There is no shame in a pupil knowing more about something than you. They could be a child prodigy or it could be their specialist subject on *Mastermind*. The trick is to embrace it, engage them and use their level of expertise to your advantage. Could they support your teaching by acting as your mini teacher, delivering elements of the topic that they are interested in? This would allow them to do extensive research, keeping them engaged in your lesson, and not providing them with an opportunity for boredom and opening the door to negative outbursts and behaviour.

What is the intent behind the action?

The only time that a pupil outsmarting you should give you cause for concern is if they are trying to use the actions to undermine you. If they are doing this, then you need to investigate the reasons why. Are they a child who requires an element of control to function? If this is the case, can you build in learning opportunities that allow them to take charge, for example, leading the class in an element in the lesson (like the mini teacher concept mentioned above)? Are they invested in being performative? We have all been around the class clown. Sometimes their actions have an element of deflection from a situation that they do not want you to hone in on, such as forgetting to do the homework task, or maybe they know they struggle to read and they don't want this to be uncovered, so they use their smart behaviour to control the narrative of the learning in your lesson. If this is the case, then you need to be on top of your differentiation and talking with your SENCO team to ensure that the correct interventions are in place to support their learning. Making that child feel capable in the lesson will be the stepping stone for them to engage more in their learning and less in disruptive behaviour.

Remain calm

A forever recurring theme, but just like before you perform any closed task, you need to take a moment to make sure that you're equipped to perform the task well. Take a breath, take a second, chuckle inwardly, then move forward. Sometimes pupils will outsmart you so perfectly that you can't be mad at them and you will have no option but to laugh.

Recognise a good game

This might seem like an odd thought process, but if you can see your pupils as a whole character and acknowledge the positive with the negative, the recognition of these negatives will begin to develop a method of identifying silver linings. Yes, it isn't great to feel outsmarted by someone younger than you, and even more so someone you are paid to impart knowledge to, but at the same time you'll be able to recognise the intelligence that they have had to put into action to be able to fulfil their outsmarting.

Gain control of the situation

It's highly likely that their peers will be witness to you being outsmarted. You don't want them to use it against you at a later date, so it's important that you are able to take control of the situation quickly and effectively. Changing the direction of attention, bringing about a sense of refocus from the action and moving on quickly will enable you to consider what your next step will be. Make sure you continue creating a positive environment without it appearing that you have lost control or that they have got a rise out of you.

Never underestimate your worthy adversary

A pupil who has gone as far as to complete the action of outsmarting you quite possibly did not just stumble across the opportunity. They will have thought about what has led them to want to outsmart you. Whether it is an experience you have shared that they have felt was negative or a power struggle situation, take the time to unpick and question why the pupil felt the need to do this in the first place. There could be an underlying issue that, if addressed, would prevent future chances of reoccurrence.

If the pupil was acting as an opportunist, however, take it at face value, find the humour, share the experience and move on, but keep your wits about you for the future!

Reflective space: So... that kid outsmarted you, huh?

If they outsmart, you can step up! Care more, give more, listen more. So, use the below space to note down your own best experience of when you've been outsmarted and ways that you'll use to deal with this happening in future.

1. What happened?

_____

_____

_____

_____

2. Was this experience personal?

_____

_____

_____

_____

3. How did the incident make you feel?

_____

_____

_____

_____

4. Is there a repeat offender involved in the situation?

_____

_____

_____

_____

5. Were there any catalysts or red flags to the incident?

_____

_____

_____

_____

6. Have you decided to take any additional steps (e.g. call home, detention, involving another member of staff)?

_____

_____

_____

_____

7. Do you feel like leaving the classroom? Why?

_____

_____

_____

_____

8. What's one thing that you would do differently if the same situation were to arise?

_____

_____

_____

_____

Chapter 5

So... you ballsed up that observation

'You've already taught us this, Miss.'
'I don't think I have, Sally Know-It-All.'
'I'm sure you have, Miss, last lesson.'
'Nope, this is something different, Tommy Shoutout.'
'Er Miss, we've already done battleship cell referencing.'
'What, Monique-Awesome-Student...?'

Names have been changed to protect the identity of the pupils, but this is a genuine interaction from back in my ITT (initial teacher training) year. I look back now and wonder how it was even possible to make the monumental balls-up that I did. I laugh to myself even more when I find my timetable at the time: one lesson on, one lesson off. Even knowing my exasperation when I realised I'd been allocated a three-lesson day. How on *earth* was I going to be able to teach three lessons in one day?! (Ha!)

I had somehow managed to get my two Year 7 lessons confused and had indeed started to teach the exact same lesson that they had had just two days earlier. I'm still not sure to this day how I managed to make it happen, but I guess that adage 'Fail to prepare, prepare to fail' fits this situation well, and somewhere along the way of trying to do time-saving planning by doubling up on lessons, I'd saved too much time by not planning this one.

Now I was faced with two options: A) admit my mistake, own it and change the task, or B) ostrich the hell out of the situation and plough on. I'd like to say I was equipped enough at this stage of my early teaching journey to have chosen option A, but because I was being observed, I was petrified of deviating from the script and also the lesson plan that I had submitted to my head of department.

I can safely say that it was a terrible decision, not to be repeated! I had lost the class, they were bored, eyes glazed, and the noisier ones had no problem with holding their own conversation, and more loudly than I could teach and deliver. I muddled through and then set them on a task that wasn't progressing them, because they had done it the other day. I'm not quite sure what I expected when the hands started raising quickly when they said the task had been completed.

And all this whilst having another well-seasoned colleague in the room, casting judgement on whether I was showing the skills needed to become a real teacher. Well, actually, I think my head of department had more than seen enough when he realised that I was going to steam through the horror show, as he put his pen and clipboard down, thanked me, and left me to get into the lovely bed I had just made for myself.

The feedback session was very quick: 'So, did you realise you'd taught that class before...?'

Consider this observation ballsed up.

Behaviours can be escalated when there is another adult in the room, both positively and negatively. A pupil's distrust of new adults can lead to your lesson observation being ruined before you've even had the chance to demonstrate your teaching capabilities. Let's not forget that there is an element of pupil behaviour and relationships in all lesson observations. It's an area that needs to be invested in early, not just for the judgement that may be received, but also because we have to appreciate that positive pupil behaviour will always contribute to positive learning experiences.

Luckily (or unluckily, depending how you look at it), I am not the only teacher to have gone through this, as Jade, Craig and Francesca kindly share their own personal balls-ups.

Case study: Jade Powers, secondary English teacher

Picture the scene: enthusiastic trainee teacher, desperate to impress her mentors; a bottom-set, extremely low-ability Year 10 class consisting of the grand total of 11 students (on a good day); last lesson on a sunny Friday afternoon in April; the need to do something 'different' and showcase my ability to 'take risks' and finally... a drama-based activity.

Yes, you guessed it. A total flop of a disaster. The messiest, clumsiest clunk of a lesson observation to date.

By this point in the year, I was feeling pretty confident with my teaching. Observations had started not to faze me so much. I'd established routines, behaviour management strategies and myself as a teacher in what was an extremely challenging school. It was an extraordinarily tough gig for your first school, but I'd risen to the challenge and managed to make significant progress with even the most disengaged of students. So, how did things go so wrong on that fateful Friday afternoon? Put simply: the need to showcase I could 'do something different' and 'take risks'. And that is precisely where everything started to go wrong.

From the beginning of the year, I had been unashamedly ambitious with this class and was determined that they were worth more than the 'Grade 2' targets they were labelled with. I had embedded strong routines into our lessons. They trusted me and knew exactly what they were going to get when they turned up at my door.

So, along came an observation and despite me knowing what worked for this class, I still felt the need to move away from my trusted routines and show that I could do something different. I was going to show I could use drama! Because of course, nothing goes together better than a fragile group of teenagers and an activity that requires the level of confidence only experienced actors possess...

I was a couple of weeks into teaching *Macbeth*. I planned a 'conscience alley'. For those (hopefully) unfamiliar with this activity, it involves students standing in two rows, hands joined to make a tunnel. One student then walks down the 'tunnel' (in this case, the student playing the role of Lady Macbeth) whilst the two rows of students chant the thoughts she might be having. It sounds simple enough... right? Wrong. The students had the knowledge to complete the task but did they have the confidence to take part in it? Of course not. Had I created an environment where drama was practised regularly and students felt safe taking part in it? Definitely not. Most importantly, was this going to help students learn or make progress in any way? Absolutely not. It was a disaster; I was helplessly throwing my arms in the air, chanting, hoping they would imitate me while instead, they stood, arms folded, glaring at me and wondering what on earth had happened to the teacher they had once trusted. Not a single student took part. I could see it wasn't working. But did I stop? Did I sensibly, swiftly move on from the activity having realised it wasn't working? No. Big mistake. And just as you would probably expect, when a group of low-ability, disengaged teenagers feel like they can't do something, they act up. The confusion turned to low-level disruption, which turned to high-level chaos. Fleets of paper aeroplanes were flying in all their glory, a chair was thrown, verbal abuse was being hurled and my voice was well and truly lost amongst it all.

Tips that I learnt? The next day, I returned to the class with my established routines and trusted tasks. Just like that, so did the calm environment that I'd spent months creating. It is important to make mistakes and try new things; this is how we learn. There is nothing wrong with trying to include drama in your lessons, or trying out new strategies or teaching styles. There is a lot wrong with doing any of this simply to try and impress, or so someone can tick a box. There is a lot more wrong with realising that any of the above isn't working and continuing with it anyway. Trust yourself and your instincts and never feel like you need to change what you do for an observation. What would I do differently today? I wouldn't have got myself into that situation in the first place. I have empathy for my students, they know that I care about them, they know that I want the best for them, and most importantly, they trust me to teach them in a way that we are all comfortable with.

But overall, I still think the biggest lesson to take away from this is that multiple adults in a room versus 11 awkward teenagers is *not* a good environment to introduce drama. Talk about stage fright!

Jade Powers is an English teacher based in the North East. It has been two years since her NQT year.

The classic advice here from Jade is that there is absolutely nothing wrong with trying something new in your lessons, but maybe an observed lesson is not the time to try it out (and by maybe, I mean, it's not!). You are already in a position where your normal learning environment is altered, just by having another adult in the room, so sticking with what is tried and tested, and using your experimental lessons for a time when you are most likely to have full control of the factors, will help prevent a MOB (monumental observational balls-up).

Case study: Craig Cunningham, associate assistant headteacher

Being an NQT was very rough for me. From day one, it felt like the odds were not stacked in my favour. I was delivering GCSE and A levels in both computer science and ICT; my A level ICT class was made up of 38 students; I was setting up the new specification for the computer science course; and the list goes on and on. The jump from PGCE to NQT was immense. In my PGCE year, I was used to getting positive feedback on my observations and being told how well I was doing. Now things had taken a complete 180 and the feedback was less than complimentary.

As I left school one evening, I mentioned to a colleague that I had an observation that coming Friday with my A level group and how the anxiety was seeping into the far-reaching corners of my mind. I was fortunate enough to have gone through the training and induction process with her, and as we boarded our train, we sat down to compare notes on our observation experiences so far. We each knew the other had done really well during PGCE, but upon discovering the lows of NQT observations, we were equally perplexed as to how the other was swan-diving into the abyss of bad observations.

Once I got home, it was clear to me that this next observation needed to be all-singing, all-dancing. I needed to wow the students and impress them with all the props and drama of a West End production, and my observer needed to know that this was my definition of a showstopper. I packed every gimmick I could into the lesson and even brought in my extremely expensive onesie in an effort to immerse the sixth-formers into coming along with me on the journey.

As I went through the motions, I thought more and more about how much of me and my personality as a teacher appeared in the lesson. I came to the conclusion that what I was doing hadn't been working so something had to change. Finally satisfied with what I'd planned, I put the lesson and myself to bed, visualising what I thought to be a masterpiece of a learning journey and how everyone would just be in awe of what I intended to deliver.

Boy, was I wrong! Observation day came around, and while delivering the lesson went according to plan, the balance was off. My students were looking at me sideways, almost suspiciously. It was as if they could smell the stunt I was trying to pull from a mile off. As I hurtled from one group to another, checking understanding, praising and signposting with differentiated cards, I noticed the observer was doing her routine walkaround to talk to students. The onesie was starting to get tighter; something was wrong. My fears were confirmed when it came to feedback. The lesson was good – it was well planned, with plenty of resources, and it considered the students' needs – but it wasn't me.

The students had commented on being used to a style of teaching from me that engaged them and that was missing from my lesson that day. The fact that some of them were disengaged became the final nail in the coffin of this lesson.

Looking back on this now, I realise that I delivered the lesson to the wrong audience. No matter who is coming into your lesson to see you do what you do, regardless of how much warning and preparation time you've had, the lesson should always be planned to your audience, and your audience are your students. They are the ones who see you all the time and get the best from you. They are the true observers.

Craig Cunningham is an associate assistant headteacher in a pupil referral unit (PRU). It has been six years since he was an NQT.

Isn't it interesting that our go-to when it comes to stepping up our teaching game is to go all-singing and all-dancing, and in turn, exhausting ourselves, killing all of our brain cells, and yet it isn't appreciated by our captive audience?! How rude! It makes you think whether it's the way to go, doesn't it? (Spoiler alert: we don't think it is, reader.)

Case study: Francesca Carr, secondary science NQT

I hit the ground running in my first year, really. Well, as much as you can do in teaching! I fell quite naturally into the routine of things, made sure to ask the oracles in my department for help when necessary, and my observations were going surprisingly smoothly! Which is why my first 'misadventure' sticks out so clearly in my mind that it will probably haunt me until I retire. (That, and the fact that my line manager reminds me of it on an almost weekly basis whilst I squirm with discomfort – thanks, Allan...).

It was my first observation with a member of the SLT – the ITT manager for our school (also an associate principal) had decided to do an official observation alongside my mentor, the aforementioned Allan. At this point, it's probably pertinent to mention my teaching philosophy – this is a term that is bandied around *a lot* during training, and basically means 'What type of teacher do you want to be?', aka 'Are you a shouty one or a pally one?' Anyway, I always knew I would be the approachable teacher, the one who cares, who has kids coming to see them at breaktimes and then crying on their last day at school because they've built up such a bond, etc. etc... it just makes sense given my personality. I'm the friend who cries with pride when you get good news, and the first one on the phone if you get worse news. I am also quite a geeky, silly person (don't worry, this is all relevant...).

Anyway, this observation rolls around, and I'm confident. As it turns out, too confident. I've settled the kids pretty smoothly. It's my dreamy, second-set Year 8s who already adore me (if I remember rightly, this was still in my first half term of teaching, but we had built rapport pretty quickly due to them being adorable and me being keen) and I'm circulating, giving out books. As an aside, I have since learnt to do this before the kids arrive, a simple but effective piece of advice, but I was still in the steepest part of my learning curve! I remember vividly (more vividly than I'd like) that I had got to the back right table in my lab, just beside where SLT Jim and mentor Allan were sitting to watch the lesson.

'Miss! It's Lydia's birthday!' comes the cry from one of the kids.

Now, Lydia is an absolute angel student, one of my favourites for sure. I know we 'don't have favourites' but let's be real here... So, as I continue to give the books out, I begin to lead the class in a rousing chorus of 'Happy Birthday'. In my head, this is brilliant, it's ingenious. I'm showing *so much* Teacher Standard 1: there is positivity *all over* this learning environment. I move on and teach a relatively uneventful lesson – I remember slight issues around timing, but that is a tricky skill to master even for an experienced teacher, so I'm pretty happy!

I manage to chase SLT Jim down later that day for my feedback (a challenge in itself), and it turns out to my abject horror that he did not share my same sunny outlook on the day's events. He absolutely rinses me for the singing (I think he may have even used the word 'unprofessional', which still turns my stomach!) and doesn't seem to have picked up on anything positive from the lesson at all, for that matter. Of course, it may just be the case that I focused so intently on my music-related shame that I blocked out or missed any constructive criticism…! And so, that's the story of how, nearly nine months later, my colleagues still occasionally sing 'Happy Birthday' to me at department meetings. Year round.

Owning up to what feels like the most epic of fails has certainly got my cheeks burning, and stirred up that shame as if it were yesterday, but I have thankfully learnt to laugh at it now. And you know what? I'd sing it again! Just absolutely under *no* circumstances in an observation… especially with the SLT!

I do get SLT Jim's point in fairness: you have to balance being this bouncy, enthusiastic, lovable teacher with the routine and structure kids desperately need, otherwise you risk doing them a grave disservice. So, I suppose that's my advice from this: that there is a time and a place for you to let that human side of you out, and timing that right will become your biggest strength. I learnt that the hard way for sure…! But at the same time, I have not and will not dull that side of myself for anyone, and my dreamy, second-set Year 8s love science because of that.

Francesca Carr is about to start her NQT year.

I think Francesca is correct here. There is always a time and a place, and you are always the adult in the room who has to be able to decide and take the lead in situations like this. But you should also remember that an observed situation and the evaluation of it can be hugely subjective. What may seem wildly inappropriate to one observer may to another demonstrate the clear rapport between a class and a teacher, a comfortable teaching style, and the key to turning what could have been a ten-minute distraction into a 45-second song and moving on back to focus. Beauty, after all, is in the eye of the beholder!

What is the purpose of lesson observations?

Teaching seems to be one of the few professions where people are invited into your working space to look over your shoulder and critique what you are doing several times a year. So, what is the purpose of us having lesson observations? If we turn to Ofsted (2018), we see that observations have been a tool for measuring standards in schools for decades: 'Lesson observation has been an important feature of the inspection process since Ofsted was founded in 1992.' Observations often use a 'high-inference model', meaning observers are required 'to make subjective inferences beyond the behaviours observed', rather than simply capturing 'observable facts or events, with minimal interpretation or subjectivity'. Ofsted also points out that 'Inspectors' use of the standardised form for collecting evidence from lesson observations has been a consistent element of practice since 1995. This has changed very little since then. The widespread perception that inspectors apply a tick-box approach is therefore contradicted by the large amount of qualitative information inspectors record from lesson observation.'

With this in mind, it's clear that drawing conclusions and making judgements based on lesson observations (rightly or wrongly) remain an integral part of the known structure of monitoring and tracking what is expected of the teaching profession, alongside being used for in-school assurance of quality-first teaching and performance management. This means that the weighting and importance that is put towards observations can have a significant toll on a teacher's mental wellbeing. It is one of those elements of teaching that you are aware of before you enter the profession – almost sold to you as an urban legend of woe, but sadly it isn't an urban legend at all because it exists!

And how does this anxiety appear? Expectations are laid out for us to deliver an outstanding lesson, but over the years there's been so much hearsay around how to achieve this that we came out with a model that means the more performative we are – the more hours of planning, the more laminating, the more we demonstrate what *we* know and can do – the better. Somehow, we lost sight of the fact that the purpose of observations is actually to demonstrate the pupils' abilities, their willingness to learn and their ability to deliver on this. All this should be seen on a consistent and daily basis via their books, their work, their actions, their outputs and their words, not just in that 20-minute snapshot of your all-singing and all-dancing demo.

In terms of a lesson observation, the Ofsted requirements are not to be able to provide a physical lesson plan, but rather to show that there is clear evidence that the lesson has been planned. They also know that lesson observation is only one tool among a range of evaluation methods for measuring teacher effectiveness and that evidence should be triangulated to make informed assessments. Ofsted (2019) look at three separate domains, one of which is behaviour:

Curriculum domain	Teaching domain	Behaviour domain
• Teachers use their subject expertise to provide effective learning opportunities. • The lesson content is appropriate to the age group and does not lower expectations. • There is a logical sequence to the lesson.	• Teachers demonstrate good communication skills. • Teachers possess good questioning skills. • Teachers give explicit, detailed and constructive feedback in class.	• Teachers create supportive classrooms focused on learning. • Pupils' behaviour contributes to the focus on learning. • There is no weighting given to any element.

The model is designed to contribute to school-level evaluation rather than evaluation of a single teacher. In that way, it sits alongside the assessment of the curriculum and impacts more effectively on the judgement of the quality of education. If you have an Ofsted inspector in your school, remember that they are not judging you individually, but evaluating the school as a whole based on a large range of criteria. Don't feel you need to put on a show for them and definitely don't try anything new!

Being observed as an NQT

Ofsted aside, you will still be observed and evaluated in your NQT year as it's statutory guidance for your teaching to be observed at regular intervals. So, do expect your NQT mentor and SLT to sit in on some of your lessons. While you shouldn't feel obliged to perform for them in any way, the thought of being observed might make you feel nervous and you don't want to balls things up like me, Jade, Craig and Francesca – if you can help it! It's worth having a think about the factors that might contribute to you messing up your observation lesson and how to avoid them.

Things to consider that could contribute to the ballsing up of your lesson:

- lack of behaviour management skills
- lack of planning
- doing too much
- not doing enough
- nerves
- lack of confidence in ability
- lack of confidence in teaching
- inability to accept a situation gone wrong
- lack of flexibility
- planning in real time
- lack of dynamic risk assessments.

It's also worth being aware that sometimes the effectiveness of your lessons can be dictated by how your school expects you to deliver and your own personality of how you deliver.

With this in mind, can we take anything from our experiences and what is expected of us, and put them together to get something of use for our playbook?

Of course we can!

Plays for the playbook

We will all have that earth-shattering moment when we discover that we are human; most people will find performing in front of an observer daunting. If you feel at ease with the person who is observing you and with (nearly) every eventuality of the way your class can respond to you and your lesson, you will feel comfortable to teach as if that person was not in the room. So, is there a way that we can set about creating an environment that you are comfortable to thrive in? Abso-bloody-lutely.

Run a game situation

This might seem like an odd one to bring to the table, but sometimes you have the ability to mirror lessons. Being able to test out something in a no-pressure environment gives you the chance to see what works and what doesn't. You can try it out across lessons for a period of time. If you know the schedule for when your observation is happening, you can even have the lessons preceding it tie in to demonstrate all that has been learnt and will continue to be learnt in future lessons.

Practise routines

As discussed in some earlier playbook moves, letting your class know what to expect from you with subtle cues to gain their attention will help you to demonstrate the command that you have of the class. This can only be achieved by running the same plays repeatedly so that it is muscle memory for those in your class. Expectations of where to find things, how to run activities and how to respond are all very important. The ability to say, 'OK, into your investigation stations', with nothing but a reminder on the board of what the groups look like and where they should be sitting, is an impressive skill for a class to achieve.

Being able to move around the class quickly and quietly can actually be developed as a competition and can be employed all the way to Key Stage 4:

> 'It took 36 seconds to get to our stations last time. Can we beat it? If we can, let's have a reward for it.'

By the time you get to your observation, you'll have conditioned those dudes like Pavlov's dogs, just by setting your verbal cue and instigating the visual cues, such as picking up your stopwatch. You don't even need to press the timer if you don't want to. The action and control are in the repetition of the prior practices.

Establish the norm

When someone comes to your lesson, they are only getting a snapshot of your learning. It's quite rare these days for an observer to stay for the duration, in fact, for more than ten to 20 minutes. This has evolved in line with Ofsted and the importance and onus being on the learning journey. This means that the most common question to be asked by an observer to a pupil in your lesson is: 'Is this what a normal lesson looks like?' The easiest way to get that answer to be the one that you want it to be, rather than be at the mercy of the child they've asked, is to make sure you've cultivated the norm so that the answer is always 'Yes'.

This can come from having a variety of set plays for certain scenarios that will come into your delivery. Whether it's a maths teacher who always has mental maths challenges at the halfway point of their lesson, an art teacher who uses peer assessment to mark and critique that lesson's work via an art gallery enactment, or a Key Stage 1 teacher who gets the handwriting Finger Gym™ equipment out and the music ready for the fine motor skills disco, knowing what your expectations are for each situation and working it through with the class means that they are not surprised whenever they are asked to enter that phase of the lesson, as it is their norm, and they know what to do.

Furthermore, this ensures a sense of safety and understanding for those with SEN or SEMH needs. You can provide them with prompts to remind and reinforce as they are aware of the outcomes that you want them to achieve, because they have done this before. Pre-learning is often their key to achieving positive outcomes.

Consistency

This is especially important when you come to observations. If you don't do the things that you usually do because there is someone else in the classroom, so that you can be seen a certain way, I promise you it will be very evident. Hell hath no fury like a child scorned, with the option to take someone down they feel has been unfair to them in a previous scenario. So, stay firm but fair, but above all, be consistent.

Don't be afraid to deviate from the plan

Sometimes. Things. Go. Wrong.
Read that again.

It's OK for it to go wrong, as long as you learn from the incident and find a way to make sure you prevent it from happening again. There will be instances where you've provided the lesson plan to your observer and it's all going belly up. Quite frankly, I think it demonstrates strength and faith in your own ability to be able to go: 'This just isn't working. We need to do something different.' Do not be tied to your lesson plan, and trust your ability to justify the need for change (if necessary). Always remember that, although there might be someone in there to see what you can do, it is still a lesson that the pupils need to take some knowledge away from. Do not sacrifice their learning for fear of being hauled over the coals for deviating from the plan that you set out.

Remember that beauty is in the eye of the beholder

I cannot stress this one enough. It has always interested me how one person's rubbish is another person's treasure. You may get an observer who believes in risk-taking and innovative and kinaesthetic lessons, and you could get another who is an advocate for quiet calm and out-of-a-textbook learning. Neither is wrong, but both are a style and an opinion. Teachers tend to teach in the manner that they themselves learn. This is because the delivery is in their comfort zone. The real trick and skill are in being able to determine the correct learning environment for the correct situation.

I'm not saying to play to what your observer likes to get a positive result (although an awareness of this helps), but I mean you should play to the style of your learners. If you have them at the heart of your decisions for the lessons, positive behaviour should come hand in hand. When delivering behaviour training, I have always likened it to getting a net to scoop up your class. Your first scoop, using a video or experiment or an example to introduce a topic, may pick up the majority of the class. Some teacher talk to consolidate what that video, experiment or example was highlighting will scoop up a few more. Giving them a chance to have a go at what you have demonstrated will hopefully scoop up the rest. If all of your teaching has the ability to deliver your information to everyone, there should be no one left behind, and no one with the opportunity to disrupt, as they have an option of accessing and enjoying the learning.

Reflective space: So... you ballsed up that observation

I imagine a lesson observation will be fairly easy for you to reflect on, especially if you are able to pinpoint classroom behaviours that made it a negative experience. We will often naturally break down all the things that went well, things that can be improved, and even the areas where we disagree with the observer. Use the space below to unpick a previous lesson observation that was impacted by behaviour. This will help you with your future planning, allowing you to identify any areas that need to be included or avoided.

1. What happened?

_____

_____

_____

_____

2. Was this experience personal?

_____

_____

_____

_____

3. How did the incident make you feel?

_____

_____

_____

_____

4. Is there a repeat offender involved in the situation?

_____

_____

_____

_____

5. Were there any catalysts or red flags to the incident?

_____

_____

_____

_____

6. Have you decided to take any additional steps (e.g. call home, detention, involving another member of staff)?

_____

_____

_____

_____

7. Do you feel like leaving the classroom? Why?

_____

_____

_____

_____

8. What's one thing that you would do differently if the same situation were to arise?

_____

_____

_____

_____

Chapter 6

So... the kids saw you outside of school

Most pupils cannot comprehend (and actually don't necessarily want to think about) the fact that their teachers have a life outside of school. If you are in a position where you are finding that there are some challenges to your behaviour management, you may want to have a stance on how you are going to tackle a scenario where your pupils see you in the local supermarket or walking down the street. While I will always take the opinion that you are the adult in the room and a certain amount of respect should be afforded to you, I also believe in not giving a class any reason to catch you on the back foot. What are you going to do if (and most likely when) they realise that you do not in fact live underneath your desk and that you are a living, breathing, contributing, socialising member of normal society? What will you do to make sure it doesn't affect your behaviour management and become detrimental in your next lesson?

When I think about the advice that I really needed in my first year of teaching, it takes me back to a period when I was an NQT and living my best life. I had been told by an older, more seasoned colleague that I was now a role model and needed to act that way, as you never know when parents or children are watching. I got into teaching to work with children and to impart knowledge, and I never appreciated the full weight of being a role model 24/7. At least, not until one bank holiday when I was on an all-day lemonade session and one of the pupils spotted me while I was enjoying my sherbets in the beer garden. I didn't even clock them until I was halfway through an anecdote that had been triggered by 'I have never', a drinking game that really should have been left in the confines of the student halls at uni. If only I knew what that wide-eyed

Year 8 from my school was thinking when he realised he was looking at six of his teachers: one draped over the table who was the strictest teacher in the school, two who clearly didn't have matching surnames but probably would eventually, or so the kissing would suggest at least, one who was swearing like a squaddie, one who was telling a story that should have had more scientific or PSHE terms in it, and one who was *gasp* smoking, but who was renowned for telling off Year 11s who had been caught doing the very same. It really wasn't unlike something from a scene in the Channel 4 TV show *Teachers* (which is also a great behaviour management tool to watch).

I'm going to cut a long story short and just say that after the parent of the Year 8 contacted the head for a discussion, the following week the head banned us from drinking in any pubs within a three-mile radius of the school, and in any pub with our staff lanyards on. As aggrieved as I was at the time, as I lived within three miles of the school and had just received a ban from all of my locals, I'm now convinced it saved untold future embarrassments.

Luckily, I'm not the only one who has been faced with very public situations that have followed them back into the classroom.

Case study: Vanessa Ward, EYFS lead

This happens a lot when you live in fairly close proximity to where you work, especially when your school is in a small village and you live in the next town that sports the closest large supermarket. Basically, this is where the parents from school come to shop. The other thing about being a primary school teacher is that kids at this age often don't hate their teachers (not blowing my own trumpet, but primary teachers are known to be pretty damn fun). So, in fact, quite the opposite is often true, and they can be a little bit obsessed with you.

At the start of my career, seeing kids in the supermarket was definitely a 'cute novelty', and of course, I was always polite, said hello and made some random small talk. However, as time went on, I realised that if a kid who knows you (and being a Reception teacher, I am the first person they are ever taught by in school, so they generally know me well) sees you in the supermarket, or engaged in any other non-school related activity, you should be prepared to be followed, have your personal space invaded and the contents of your shopping basket narrated out loud for all to hear.

Knowing this was how it worked, I decided from now on, when I saw a kid and parent I knew in the supermarket, there was only one thing for it: avoid by any means. Because if they see you, one of two scenes will inevitably play out:

Scene 1

Child: 'Hi Mrs Ward! Look, Mummy, it's Mrs Ward!'
The parent, who is deep in concentration deciding which curry sauce to put in her basket, briefly looks over.
Parent: 'Oh hi, you alright?'
We exchange a polite acknowledgement of one another then carry on studying the rice... microwave or boil in the bag? The child then continues to follow me for the rest of the shopping trip.

Scene 2

It's Friday night and it's been a long week. Can you guess which supermarket aisle I've come to as a priority? I reach out for my second bottle of wine – buy one get one half price, great!
Child: 'Hi Mrs Ward!'
Oh ffs, have they actually followed me here?
Me *(putting on my best enthusiastic teacher voice)*: 'Oh hello Emily. Are you being super helpful doing the shopping with Mummy?'
Child: 'Yeah! How many bottles of wine are you getting, Mrs Ward? What kind of pizza is that? I love pizza!'
Just wonderful...

So, the supermarket is a fairly normal place to get 'spotted' by a kid who knows you from school. Everyone's got to eat, right? But my most recent experience takes this to another level.

In my spare time, I am a keen hockey player, and I enjoy taking part in regular training sessions and matches that take place at a local secondary school, which has an indoor sports centre and swimming pool linked to it. Unfortunately, during the winter months, it isn't unusual for our matches to end up being postponed due to water-logged or frozen pitches. This was the case one particular Saturday, so it was arranged for us to play some indoor hockey in the sports hall. We were about to start our session, when I noticed two familiar faces smiling, waving and trying to get my attention through the window. It was two pupils (siblings aged nine and seven) who attend the school I now work at. Lovely! I politely smiled and waved back.

When the session was over, I headed to the women's changing rooms to grab a shower. Upon entering, I realised that a kid's swim session must have just finished at around the same time as ours. Whose voice did I then hear?

Child from the window: 'Hello Mrs Ward!'

Great... just great.

Now normally, as a 'well-seasoned' hockey player, I would just strip off and get straight in the shower – I'm definitely not shy! But this would clearly be rather inappropriate. So, I dawdled, hoping that they would finish before I needed to get naked. They didn't. Marvellous. And I was in a rush! So I flipped back into my body-conscious teenage self and tried all the techniques for getting changed under a towel without revealing myself. I managed to get down to my underwear safely and basically ran for the shower. Luckily there were cubicles with doors!

Thankfully the voices in the changing room diminished as I was showering. Maybe I was safe? But as I hung my underwear over the top of the door...

Child from the window: 'Look Mummy, Mrs Ward's having a shower! And look, there's her pants!!'

So... a kid saw me outside of school, trying to avoid accidentally getting naked in front of them.

Vanessa Ward is an EYFS lead in a primary school. She has been teaching for ten years since being an NQT.

I'm sure we're all cringing in unison, and I can only thank Vanessa for providing us with an anecdote that is so far down the embarrassment spectrum that anything we do now will feel like small fry in comparison.

We need educators like Vanessa, for keeping it real and also for finding the humour in a situation that some may think humourless.

Case study: Vivienne Porritt, former secondary headteacher

Throughout my teaching career, I lived as far away as possible from the school. There was a reason for this which stemmed from one moment in my first year of teaching. It is still a moment I relive in my nightmares!

I was an excited and, in hindsight, naive new teacher and I must have missed the PGCE lecture that advised us on meeting students out of school. If you don't recall that advice either, let me explain why it's essential so that future new teachers are spared what happened to me.

After my first week of teaching, I needed to buy an outfit as I had been invited to a wedding. Following five years at university, I didn't have anything in my wardrobe suitable for a wedding. My new teacher outfits weren't suitable either as I had bought them to look grown up, which was not the look I wanted at the wedding. So, on the Saturday of my first week as a grown-up, I headed to the shops in the small town where my school was based. I wanted to look sexy and yet stylish on very little money, as I wouldn't be paid for several weeks. I headed to the shop which would meet all the criteria: Topshop to the rescue, I thought.

What could go wrong? Groups of girls laughing that their new teacher was in their shop? Trying to buy some clothes but I had forgotten my purse so cue more girls laughing? Buying the same outfit as one of my new 15-year-old students?

Much, much worse!

It is funny now, as I'm delighted to meet previous students. Last Christmas, I met a group from my first class in that first school and it was joyous. We are all grown-ups now and reminisced about my attempts to make them laugh and the ways they sometimes embarrassed me in class. And then I was reminded of the moment that almost made me give up teaching and rush home to the North of England.

Back to the wedding outfit I was looking for! Topshop had several promising outfits and I headed for the changing rooms with armfuls of clothes. Of course it was a communal changing room, in common with all the shops in which I had bought clothes as a student.

I worked my way through my choices, leaving the one I hoped was perfect to the end. I'll describe it for you as every moment is burned into my retina. It was a two-piece, with a cream, pleated dress and a see-through floral cover-up. It was gorgeous and I could look stylish for the wedding yet take off the top for the party afterwards. The top of the dress had spaghetti straps – very thin straps to the uninitiated. That meant I couldn't wear a bra under the dress as it would have shown through the cover-up and we definitely didn't show our bras then! I was bothered what that would look like; it was thin material. To be very clear: would people be able to see my boobs at the evening party?

You will now have worked out what happened. To test whether my boobs would show or not, there was only one option. It was something I'd been comfortable doing whilst clothes-shopping and had never given it a second thought. So, I took my bra off and began to put the dress on by raising my arms for the dress to come over my head.

I'm stood there, half-naked, with my arms raised so my boobs took on more prominence than usual. At precisely this moment, I heard a girl's voice say, 'Isn't that our new teacher?'

Reader, I froze.

I had the dress covering my face so couldn't see who was speaking. Then the suppressed laughter started. It sounded as if there were a hundred of them, so loud were the giggles. I didn't know whether to pull the dress down or take it off as I realised they were going to watch either way. I pulled the dress down, put on the cover-up and looked in the mirror as if pondering whether to buy it. I was going to stay in that changing room in that dress until the shop shut, if necessary. So, I'm pirouetting in front of the mirror and the girls are laughing louder.

In the end they cracked first. They walked out of the changing room in single file to prolong my agony. The last girl paused, looked me in the eyes and said, 'It's lovely, Miss', and ran out.

What happened when I walked into their class the next week may need to be another chapter!

Vivienne Porritt is Vice President of the Chartered College of Teaching and a strategic leader of #WomenEd. Previously she was a secondary headteacher and Director of School Partnerships at UCL Institute of Education.

So far, nudity seems to be the theme of pupils seeing us outside of school (I'm with you in wondering how I managed to get two anecdotes in this category!) but now I'm going to hand over to Kemi to help us end on some sort of dignified note...

Case study: Kemi Oloyede, head of science

The thought of seeing my students outside of school used to make me cringe. I don't work too far from where I live, so my biggest fear was my students knowing my address. Thankfully that has never happened, touch wood.

But let's take it back for a moment. Remember when you were in primary school and you'd see your favourite teachers outside of school? No? Just me? OK, moving on. Well, I was actually happy to see them and they seemed happy to see me, even if they were putting up a front. I wasn't the perfect student, but the kindness they showed me in school as well as outside of school had a lasting impact on me and made me want to be a better student.

Let's fast forward to the present day. You're now a teacher yourself and you bump into your students outside of school, so what do you do? It's like the fight or flight response. Sometimes there's an awkward smile, pause or conversation, or sometimes the conversation can be easy, calm and pleasant. Or do you act like you haven't seen your student at all and vice versa?

During my training year, I saw my favourite Year 10 class in Westfield (I know you're not supposed to have favourites, so don't judge me). It was the summer holidays and I was meeting with some friends. I wore a vest top and a skirt that stopped above my knees. I have to give you the details of what I wore because I worked in a Jewish school, which had a large cohort of black students. Anyway, I was in a world of my own, walking towards where I'd meet my friends, and out of nowhere I heard, 'Miss O! Miss O!' Before I could even turn around, I had about seven of my students run up to me and hug me. They were so happy to see me. Now like I said before, the thought of seeing students outside of school used to make me cringe, but I was happy to see them. Seeing their faces warmed my heart and brought a smile to my face. What did make me cringe though, was when one of the girls said, 'Miss, you're showing your shoulders and your skirt is above your knee… that's not kosher.' (Working in the Jewish school meant I had to cover my shoulders and legs.) We all burst out laughing and another student chimed in, 'Miss is young, you know, and this isn't school. She can wear what she wants.' That encounter with my students broke the ice with them in a way that teaching them in a classroom didn't during my training year. During my NQT year my relationship with those girls blossomed. I can honestly say I hardly had to deal with 'bad behaviour' and I became their mentor. This was almost seven years ago and I'm still a mentor to two of those girls today.

Let me tell you the pros and cons of seeing your kids outside of school.

Pros:

- They now see you as human. You have a life outside of work too and sometimes students forget that. So, it's good for them to be reminded.
- You get to see them in a different environment. See how they act, behave and conduct themselves outside of the classroom. Maybe this could help you to understand them better.
- Common interests. Maybe you see them while you're out shopping or in a restaurant. This gives you some leverage maybe to find some common ground or mutual interests, and this will help you to build a better relationship with them.

Cons:

- God forbid they ever see you go into your house. I'd rather my students not know where I live.
- Caught in the act. You might see one of your students involved in something that they shouldn't be doing outside of school. Especially if the student is at risk, you will have to inform the police and your DSL or contact parents, and this could be stressful, especially if this is supposed to be your time but you're still worrying about your student. We are more than teachers and our care goes beyond the school gates.

Kemi Oloyede is a head of science and SENCO, and the founder of the Young Black Teachers Network. It has been five years since her NQT year.

So, is it the end of the world to be spotted outside of school by pupils? In most circumstances not only is the answer no, but also it is almost impossible to avoid. Most teachers take proximity of a school into their decision-making when it comes to choosing a place of work. I know that I have personally lived within walking distance of three of my schools. This has both played in my favour and gone against me.

It is important to stay mindful though of the situations that we can unconsciously place ourselves into. And also, remember that it cuts both ways. Pupils may equally not be as keen to see you, because time outside of school and away from parental supervision is a time for them to let loose, and seeing you could be a horrifying prospect for them!

Plays for the playbook

If you don't take the opportunity to handle these events, you may find that they interfere with your teaching. A pupil revealing mid-lesson that they saw you on Saturday night is always a sure-fire way to distract from the learning outcomes and lead to unnecessary discussions (especially if two out of the three contributions that we had in this chapter are anything to go by). Taking control of the narrative from the beginning will help with this, especially if we look to our playbook for some pointers.

Peak shopping and socialising times

While you cannot and should not hide away, if you are concerned about being around pupils outside of school, may I suggest patronising local 24-hour shops or even better, shopping online, because, unless you are related to your pupils, they would have a really tough time explaining why they were in your living room whilst you're minding your own business filling up your ASOS shopping basket.

Unfortunately, you are on the same schedule as they are, so it is highly likely that they will be in the same shopping centres, leisure centres, bowling alleys and restaurants as you, especially during the holidays. Even more so if you have your own family who may want to use the soft play, the parks and local farm. It is just a case of planning in advance to be able to move on quickly, so that you can continue your day, even if you keep on bumping into each other. For example: 'Lovely to see you, Illy. Can't wait to see you on Monday and you can tell me all the fun you've had then.' 'Huxley, looks like great minds think alike. How about you enjoy your day and I'll enjoy mine and we'll pretend we didn't see each other.' (Think about saying this more with a friendly smile *à la* Miss Honey in *Matilda* rather than a grimace akin to Mr Gilbert in *The Inbetweeners*.) If the chat does return to the classroom, I would suggest quietly offering them an option: 'You seem quite keen to discuss this, and seeing as it was something that happened outside of school time, maybe you'd like to continue this discussion then too. No? How about at break time? No? You sure? OK, let's get back to the learning then.'

Will you challenge behaviour when you are out?

In most cases, as much as you don't want to see a pupil, they most probably don't want to see you either, so there is a chance that you will both have a knowing nod and disperse your separate ways, only to tell your respective pals, 'You'll never guess who I saw today.' (Insert your more appropriate pupil prose for the same sentiment.)

But what about those situations where it is a bit more difficult to ignore seeing a pupil, for example, where a group of your pupils is acting up on a bus, causing issues to members of the public?

As with every scenario, you have to gauge the mood. Children do tend to feel a lot braver when they have several friends around them, but in most instances, a reality check without embarrassing them, but also letting them know that their actions could have some consequences, might do the trick. If they are in their uniform, it makes it a lot easier to intervene. Try scripts such as, 'I would really prefer that you didn't decide to bring that poor behaviour to the public whilst wearing our tie so proudly' or 'I'm sure the whole bus would appreciate it if you could bring the level down a bit. I've seen you know how to do it when we're in school, so it'd be nice to demonstrate it now.' A simple reminder that you know them is sometimes enough too: 'Mr Smith... shall we talk about this on Monday?' Once they realise there is a certain amount of accountability to being recognised, they tend to curtail their behaviour. It is much easier to be poorly behaved when there are no ramifications.

Social media presence

With our ever-changing and evolving world, we are more present than ever on social media (especially as I am writing this in lockdown from COVID-19). I have come across staff who take different stances, and while I would say that none are incorrect, being an ICT teacher, more than once have I overheard the glee of mischievous typing when pupils have discovered a picture of a teacher after looking up their name on a search engine. All, thanks to blocking software, have been appropriate, and usually from a snippet from an online newspaper for some amateur sports, leading said member of staff to opt some bragging rights and be conservative with the truth when they explain, 'Yes, that's correct. I could have played for England, but Elliot Daley put a high tackle on me when we were in the U10s England academy and that concussion ended all my chances.'

My point is, it isn't difficult for our increasingly tech-savvy pupils to pull up information on you if they feel the desire to, but you do have a hand in allowing them to see only what you want them to. Make sure you do the following:

- Check your privacy settings.
- Limit who can access your social media pages just by searching your name.
- Choose where to use your name online or whether to have an alias or username that doesn't link to you.
- Explain to your friends about how your online presence needs to be, so if there are likely to be pictures you don't want others to see, ask them not to tag you.
- Do not have pupils as friends on your social media, but also be aware if there is a staff member who does, you may not want to be their online friend, as they can become the link allowing the pupils they have added (but you have not) to see into your virtual world.

- Pupils will try to add you, so explain to them in person that you will always make time for them in school, but it wouldn't be appropriate for you to have them on your social media.

There is no harm in pupils seeing you outside of school, but ultimately, make sure that the version they do see of you doesn't have the ability to undermine your work with them during school time. You often only get one opportunity to build your character and reputation, so make sure it is the one that you want to be maintained.

Reflective space: So... the kids saw you outside of school

Is it the end of the world that they have seen you outside of school? Absolutely not, but let's get that experience down on paper and start thinking about how we can work it into a positive and prevent any repeat of the negatives.

1. What happened?

_____

_____

_____

_____

2. Was this experience personal?

_____

_____

_____

_____

3. How did the incident make you feel?

_____

_____

_____

_____

4. Is there a repeat offender involved in the situation?

_____

_____

_____

_____

5. Were there any catalysts or red flags to the incident?

_____

_____

_____

_____

6. Have you decided to take any additional steps (e.g. call home, detention, involving another member of staff)?

_____

_____

_____

_____

7. Do you feel like leaving the classroom? Why?

_____

_____

_____

_____

8. What's one thing that you would do differently if the same situation were to arise?

_____

_____

_____

_____

Chapter 7

So... you thought you'd planned the perfect lesson

In my early teaching years, I'd got the memo somewhere that in order to be a good teacher, you had to be an all-singing, all-dancing, performing one-woman band. After all, the more that was going on, the more engaged and interesting your lessons would be, right? I would plan and plan the night before, particularly for an observation, making hundreds of new resources and throwing in new teaching methods I'd just read about into the melting pot. I would finish observations in a flurry, just short of panting out of breath with my arms raised waiting for my applause, akin to a gymnast who had just finished a particularly energetic routine.

In one instance, I remember thinking that I had achieved an outstanding lesson and sat waiting for my head of department to bestow well-deserved praise, only to be greeted by a raised eyebrow and the question, 'So, do you think they all achieved the learning outcome?'

'Of course,' I replied incredulously, although now I was a little wrong-footed and not quite as confident as I had been. Had my underperforming boys really engaged with the content? Were those girls staring at me with adoration for a love of coding, or were they actually glazed over?

'Sometimes, Miss,' my head of department trod carefully, as I'm sure he knew he had the potential to break the spirit of a new teacher, 'less is more. I have no doubt that you are... enthusiastic for the subject, but I'm not so sure that the progress in the lesson is measurable. Some of those pupils looked a little lost on how the learning objective matched the activity, as was I. Am I right that you hadn't done some of those activities with them before today?'

Looking back, that lesson was actually chaotic. It did jump around all over the place, lost focus, but more importantly, lost pupil interaction, their effort and maybe even their need to engage their brain, all in the name of a fun observation.

Now I like to spend the first few months with my classes training them. They know where to go if they need to stretch and challenge themselves. I am able to project the activity onto the board and they go and fetch what's needed and get on with it, rather than seeing 'collaborative learning paper aeroplanes' and being met with blank faces. I want them to understand the routines of their learning so that they are able to be accountable and take responsibility for moving themselves forward. Funnily enough, once this started to happen with this particular class, I began to see an improvement in their homework and self-directed work too. They were no longer passive and were becoming independent thinkers and learners, and able to demonstrate this on a regular basis, with or without my input. Once a term, I challenge myself to see how little I can do in a lesson because it shows me how much they are actually taking on and learning. Sometimes I even get one of them to take the lesson. I can keep it fun, punchy and engaging without putting on a matinee performance.

Planning will very much reinforce positive behaviour outcomes. If you have ever winged a lesson that you know you really shouldn't have, you will remember how everything that could go wrong probably did. It wouldn't take a genius to figure out that most of the issues stemmed from a lack of preparation and planning.

Planning sets out clear expectations from the beginning of how you want your lesson to run. The time that you take to think about what you are delivering will also allow you to identify any potential red flags before they happen. Although hindsight helps us a lot, planning gives us the opportunity for foresight in understanding our pupils and what areas of our topic may bring about behaviours that we might want to have more control over. For example, open-ended activities with more freedom may not be suited to certain pupils, so they may need a task sheet to keep them focused or they may need to work with other adults who are in your classroom during that lesson.

But as is not surprising, I am not the only one who has been on that impossible mission to achieve lesson-planning perfection, as Rebekah and Harriet can testify to.

Case study: Rebekah Akroyd, PhD student and RE practitioner

Midway through my NQT year, I was starting to feel pretty confident about including a wider variety of activities in my lessons. Following advice from my mentor, I had planned a vibrant and engaging lesson for my Year 7 RE class about Christian places of worship. Rather than just reading about the different objects important to Christians, the class would be out of their seats and taking part in a treasure hunt to find the different objects – some as pictures, some as physical items. I'd been nervous about this, but in the previous lesson we'd talked about the importance of respecting religious objects, so I was feeling quite confident it would be OK. Like many teachers, I suffer from perfectionitis, so I had lined up five different activities to ensure 100 per cent engagement and zero opportunities for off-task behaviour for the next 60 minutes.

As I greeted the class at the door, handing out a starter wordsearch containing the Christian artefacts we would be looking for that lesson, I whizzed through the lesson in my mind: wordsearch, video clip about churches and Christian worship, treasure hunt, opinion line and then a reflective writing task. I spotted Abu sliding into the wrong seat. Abandoning my post at the door, I headed over to quietly remind him of the seating plan. Several minutes of negotiating and outlining of consequences later, he was in the correct seat. I reminded the class they had two minutes left to complete the wordsearch. After a few minutes of technical glitches to the tune of 'Refresh the page, Miss!', while the class watched the rest of the video clip, I nipped around the room hiding a few more pictures and objects for them to find for the main task. Some pupils started to lean across the aisle, chatting to each other. I paused the video and reminded them of my expectations. We need to stay on task because there's so much to get done, I told them, feeling increasingly panicky about the time myself. With the clip finished and the class all hunting for Bibles, rosary beads, crosses, stoles, statues and so on, I stood at the front, awarding praise points to pupils who had described six or more artefacts. Great, this was really keeping them on task. 'I can't do it,' Usman complained to me. Quickly telling him to stop wasting time, I headed over to a noisy corner of the room.

Niamh and Ismail were shouting at each other, whilst Janine repeatedly asked, 'Miss, Miss, I've only got four things. Where are the others?' Trying to speak to all three at once, I spotted Frank out of the corner of my eye peering under all the chairs in the room. 'Miss, Miss, we can't find any icons,' chorused three girls hovering next to me.

Somewhat exasperated, I reiterated the need to look carefully and to describe at least six items or consequences would apply. 'But I've only got five. It's not fair,' moaned Mia next to me. Surveying the organised chaos, my eyes passed over my bag. Sticking out of the top I could see a Bible... whoops.

While my heart was in the right place in planning engaging activities for my class, I now realise I overlooked two key issues for behaviour management. These are: being flexible and thinking about what pupils are learning, rather than what tasks they are doing. These days I would go for a simpler approach, maybe using a recall task as a starter before the treasure hunt, which could emphasise opportunities for comparisons with other places of worship we had learnt about, creating a sense of continuity for the class. Simplifying the lesson would allow more time for exploring the purpose of the activities with the class, so that they would be engaged because of their enthusiasm for learning about the topic, not just with the activities themselves. Here, I didn't have my own classroom, so I juggled setting up with managing the start of my lesson. Now, I'd save a treasure hunt for a time when I could set it up properly during breaktime and give my full attention to the class, avoiding the chaos that ensued.

I've also realised that planning the perfect lesson isn't just about having the ideas; it's about being flexible and ready to adapt. I sensed that things were going wrong in this lesson and started to feel flustered about the time. No doubt the class also sensed that I was a bit on edge. It would have been much better to have responded to the situation in front of me by spontaneously cutting out an activity, or pausing the class briefly to assess why they were struggling to complete the work, rather than blindly continuing to the next task.

Rebekah Akroyd is a PhD student in education and a RE practitioner. It has been three years since her NQT year.

Resources can be our biggest contributor to a successful lesson, but when we lose them or they're used incorrectly, they can be a factor towards opportunities for poor behaviour (shouting out, disengagement and distraction to name a few!).

Case study: Harriet Farnham, head of English

The strategies don't work. At least, this was the conclusion I had dejectedly come to by the end of the autumn term of my NQT year teaching English in South London. Heading into my second year of teaching, I was impatient to implement all of the exciting strategies I had been too burnt out to introduce the year before. My new schemes of work were bursting with Socratic debates, drama lessons, dialogic talk, and creative group work – all underpinned by the latest pedagogical theories, of course. I had, after all, believed my tutors when they told me that meticulous planning was the key to a happy classroom.

After a term of bells-and-whistles lessons, however, I had to admit that nothing I had tried to implement with my Year 9s was working. I was convinced that I had done everything by the book: clear expectations, scaffolding, differentiation, careful timing and consistency. With an almost impressive reliability, however, the activities I planned always resulted in the students hissing verbal abuse at each other.

My Year 9s had seemingly returned from the summer holidays having undergone some kind of twisted personality adjustment surgery. My sweet, shy, self-conscious students from the year before had been replaced by children the size of adults, incapable of removing the expressions of disgust that stretched across their faces whenever another student spoke.

The class was a 'nurture' group for SEN students, many of whom I had taught the year before and had solid relationships with. Frustrated with how we seemed to be going backwards, I called in the help of our wonderful educational psychologist. I was certain that she could provide some strategies to help me better meet the needs of my SEN pupils. However, after her lesson observation she told me, 'You're doing absolutely everything right teaching- and learning-wise, but your students aren't collaborating. They clearly don't get on and you need to address that first.' I was so deflated. Wasn't collaboration exactly what

I was trying to foster through my zany group activities? Didn't she know that teenagers were horrible to each other?

As it turns out, the educational psychologist was completely right. Embarrassingly, it took a near health and safety disaster for me to admit it.

One hot afternoon in spring term, the Year 9s were about to leave for lunch when we realised that the new electric door system had broken and we were trapped inside the classroom. It will come as no surprise to those of you working in new academy buildings that it took almost 50 minutes for us to be let out. Hot, frustrated and gutted to be missing jerk chicken day in the canteen, my students began hurling insults at each other. This was going to be a long lunch break.

I decided to put a world map up on the board and ask students to point to a place that meant something to them and explain why. We all got to know each other better during that lunch break than we had in nearly a year and a half together. Students shared stories about grandparents in different countries, special holidays and trips, the languages they speak at home, memories of family members passed, and moving migration stories.

I can honestly say that the near-traumatic experience of being stuck in a smelly classroom with 14 teenagers was the best thing that could have happened to my teaching approach. I realised that, in accounting for every precious minute of class in my lesson planning, I had failed to make time to simply listen to the young people in my classroom. We all needed to get to know each other a little better before I stood a chance of pulling off a Socratic circle.

After that, I began inviting the students' families to come into school to watch short performances, poetry readings and look through books. When school was too hectic to arrange parent visits, I sent videos and photos home instead. We still had our bad days, but now, for the most part, when students were faced with group work in the drama room, they worked more seriously to pull off their projects. When someone finished a presentation, the others would clap instead of shouting 'wasteman'. When we did peer feedback, students would offer meaningful suggestions rather than drawing genitalia.

Through struggling to implement strategies that I really believed in, I learnt that pedagogy alone doesn't result in good teaching. There wasn't anything wrong with the strategies I was trialling, but to give them a chance, I really needed to address a deeper problem with my classroom environment first.

My tips to you would be:

- ask for help
- get creative with parental engagement
- try to determine the root of the problem
- keep it simple; sometimes you don't need bells-and-whistles lessons
- remember that ups and downs are part of the process.

Harriet Farnham is a head of English and it has been three years since she was an NQT.

Seeking external help can be incredibly useful when you have reached the bottom of your pot of ideas as to how to keep your lesson being successful, when there is a clear case of disruption taking away from a successful learning environment. Harriet was right here to step it up by looking into what I call 'stakeholder support' – in other words, looking to those who are invested in positive outcomes for the pupils involved, in this case the educational psychologist and the parents. Her tips about it taking time to implement strategies are also incredibly valid but sometimes difficult, especially if you feel that time isn't on your side so you need to get an immediate response to your changes.

So, I guess the question we need to ask here is: is it even possible to plan the perfect lesson? And if the answer is no, then why do we get that warm, smug emotion as we Conor McGregor strut to the classroom thinking that we have nailed it and nothing could possibly go wrong?

Planning the 'perfect' lesson

Fail to prepare. Prepare to fail. I know I've already said this but it doesn't hurt to drill the sentiment in at any stage of your teaching career. If you haven't heard it yet, I'd like to know the rock that you've been living under and whether there is room for me, as it must be super cosy and soundproof!

The reason that we can trick ourselves into the illusion of having planned the perfect lesson is because you feel you have achieved this by precisely planning 50 to 110 minutes that cover all bases:

- Differentiation? Got it.
- Stretch and challenge? Nailed it.
- Innovation and engagement? But of course.
- Assessment for learning? Don't insult me.
- Keywords, literacy and numeracy infusion? Do bears poop in the woods?
- EAL translations and trigger pictures? Yep yep.
- SEN social stories? Yes, in images.
- Punchy plenary? Floated like a butterfly and stung like a bee.
- Perfect lesson? Completed it, mate.

Surely if you nail all of these and cover all of these bases, it will leave no gaps for poor behaviour to sneak in?

As you can see, and no doubt already know, there is such a multitude of factors that happen in a classroom that will determine whether a teacher gets their lesson objectives across (and I haven't even added lesson objectives onto that list above!). In order for you to be able to plan a lesson that delivers and captures learning for all, there is so much to take on. So, imagine doing all of that work, that planning, that printing and laminating, finding the perfect images, the font, the constant thought processes, only to have a student derail your lesson.

Sounds horrifying, and yet it can happen. And one derailed moment in a lesson can lead very quickly to a derailed day.

So what, if anything, can we do to minimise the demoralisation of a perfect lesson being far from that?

To have the perfect plan A means you need to have a foolproof plan B. Something to go to when things just aren't going your way. As we all know, you could do an activity with a class in one lesson and then do the exact same activity in the exact same way the following week, and it completely falls flat on its face. You can't fathom for the life of you what has altered. All external factors in your opinion have remained the same, or so you thought. You didn't realise that they had an assembly first thing with a rambunctious theatre group that left them wound up like coils only for them to unspring in your lesson, taking that perfect lesson with them.

Plays for the playbook

In terms of plays, I think we need to take a completely different tack in this chapter and be purely reflective. You see, as I mentioned before, and keep mentioning because it is my mantra and I think you should make it yours, especially on those days when you feel like you're not as good a teacher as the next person, beauty is in the eye of the beholder, and so too is perfection (or the striving towards it), and your lesson is going to be measured in different ways. It's also worth mentioning that what may look like 'perfection' in one school or key stage may not look the same in another.

If I'm honest, I'd like you to get the notion of perfection out of your head. Hold yourself to high standards, yes, but perfection could lead you to a state of self-torment, self-loathing and self-pressure, all for a result that could be impossible to achieve. With high standards comes the ability to have room for improvement, as although we are the teachers, we should also be forever learning. With perfection comes the idea that you have the ability to be the finished article and therefore have nothing more to learn, change or grow.

How do you measure engagement in your lesson?

Is it a one-size-fits-all approach that you take? Do you feel that if the class is quiet for the entirety of your lesson, this demonstrates that they are involved, engaged and learning? I personally am an advocate for a controlled buzz when you are teaching. Being able to create an environment where pupils are in control of their learning, but also able to ask questions to their peers and yourself without fear of repercussion or accusations of disruption, is the vibe that I try to establish.

I find that you can gauge the level of involvement by including assessment for learning (AfL) tactics and dropping mini plenaries throughout your teaching. By actively assessing learning, you will constantly have a sense of how much the pupils have grasped and how to continue to challenge their learning. This means that the lesson objectives or outcomes that you have been trying to achieve are subject to a 'dynamic risk assessment' throughout, resulting in less likelihood of a lesson getting away from you.

Do you have a way of moderating your planning? Are role models or exemplar planning in your area available to you?

Most ITT providers will provide you with their tried and tested way of recording your lesson planning. Many teachers continue to use these throughout their career, rarely adapting or changing them, unless they are told by their setting that they have to use a specific one. As you go on through your career, you'll find that the physical recording of your planning may become less and less, even getting to the stage where a sentence in your teacher planner is enough. I would strongly suggest, whatever your experience of teaching, that you revisit options that are out there. A lot of planning tools can be done on one page and have the ability to provide the trigger that you require to make sure that your fishing net of learning scoops up all the participants of your lesson.

List the areas that are important for you to scoop in a specific class. Even if you find that you add a small box called 'focus' because you have a child with an EHCP and ADHD whose attention span does not go beyond four minutes and you need to jot down ten ideas to keep him engaged. This niche part of your personal lesson planning will help contribute to that high-standard lesson that you are after.

What is your previous experience with that class? Can you take anything from that lesson and into the next?

We live and learn, right? But do we really?! If we all know that the definition Albert Einstein gave us of insanity is doing the same thing over and over and expecting different results (side bar: Albert Einstein did not in fact say this, but it backs up my thought process too much for me not to use it and fake credit him!), then could it be said that sometimes we do not seriously evaluate what we are doing as teachers and happily plough on and repeat it, safe in the assumption that it was the class that did not respond well and nothing to do with our execution of teaching the topic?

Sometimes, certain elements of delivery just do not work with certain ages, stages and genders. There is nothing wrong with this: as we all know, one size does not fit all. This is not to say that what went wrong in one lesson could not be used and tried with another.

Keeping notes of your own personal WWW, EBI (*internal shudder*, but if it ain't broke… for the people in the back who missed that in Pedagogy 101, it stands for What Went Well, Even Better If) will enable you to see at a glance what is something you could revisit and what is something that, quite frankly, shouldn't be touched again with a barge pole!

How much are *you* doing and how much are *they* doing?

I refer you back to my anecdote. There is such a thing as doing too much. After all, if you were to ask anyone for 'classic lines that all teachers say', I can promise you that 'I have my qualifications, it's you who needs yours' will occupy a top five spot. With that in mind, should you be working harder than the pupils to achieve the learning? I am a strong believer that a lot of personal growth and learning from children comes from the ability to take responsibility for their own learning.

Is there too much going on for one lesson? All action, no learning?

In my experience, the pursuit of the perfect lesson tends to mean that all sorts of things have been thrown in. A quick piece of advice for this one: treat your lesson like accessorising an outfit. When putting on an outfit, take off the last thing that you put on (Coco Chanel). Your enthusiasm at fitting in all the exciting things you have for the lesson could result in you trying to fit too much in for the time you have, meaning that you may ending up robbing Peter to pay Paul and resulting in the lesson not making all the sense that it would have done in its entirety. Try and be succinct in your planning and always remember: what is not used in one lesson can roll over into another.

Does student voice help inform your planning?

It always surprises me how student voice is mainly done as a whole-school activity. Why wait for a student council meeting when you have access to your own council on a daily basis? There are many ways you can do this: a digital class survey on the board where votes can be sent in; a discussion on what and how they've enjoyed learning; or a survey for them to fill out for homework. Want real honesty? Anonymise your class, but put on your thick-skin jacket first. Let's not forget that kids can be brutal! The thing to take from this exercise is that, regardless of age, pupils can be very articulate on how they like to learn and you may be surprised that they don't all ask to sit outside under a tree. While teaching is getting more and more innovative, one of the hardest lessons that I had to learn was that some pupils really enjoy learning from a textbook. This was a totally alien concept to me as it is the opposite of how I personally like to learn, meaning that it didn't align with my teaching ethos, but it helped improve knowledge and understanding among those who requested it and worked well alongside my teaching, so win win.

All of these musings, if answered well, will contribute to positive behaviour management techniques by a secondary intervention: solid lesson planning. While it may not be a primary step for improving behaviour, the off-shoots of successful implementation will contribute towards a positive, focused and progressive learning environment that reduces opportunities for pupil distraction and negative behaviours to creep in.

Reflective space: So... you thought you'd planned the perfect lesson

Instead of the usual reflective questions you've been answering in other chapters in this book, try these bespoke questions about lesson planning. Think about a lesson that you thought you had planned meticulously but that took a turn for the worse when you actually started teaching it.

1. What happened?

_____

_____

_____

_____

2. What made you think this lesson was going to be perfect?

_____

_____

_____

_____

3. Did you really plan for every eventuality?

_____

_____

_____

_____

4. Are you a reflective practitioner?

_____

_____

_____

_____

5. Is striving for perfection leaving you no margin for error or improvement?

_____

_____

_____

_____

6. Did the lesson go as poorly as you thought it did? Or is it just your perception?

_____

_____

_____

_____

7. What is your method of recording your planning?

_____

_____

_____

_____

8. How do you evaluate whether the learning outcomes have been met?

_____

_____

_____

_____

Chapter 8

So... you have a great method to reward and sanction

I just could not motivate this class to work. I had inherited a Year 11 business studies class, and I thought that my vibrant, innovative lesson plans would be enough to get them engaged and on board, and if that didn't work, they were in Year 11, so by default they would be self-motivated and ready to earn their grades. Oh, the naivety of a trainee teacher.

It was hard enough that they were a group of boisterous boys, but they only seemed to behave when their actual teacher (who remained sat at her desk throughout my lessons, maybe for fear of them ripping me limb from limb in her absence) flashed them a look that quickly and clearly transmitted the message, 'Throw that again, I dare you.' I was very much ready for the stage of my teaching career when I had mastered my 'teacher glare' but I was not there yet.

This class had been causing me some sleepless nights, but I had reread my Bill Rogers, rewatched my *Supernanny* and revisited *It's Me or the Dog*. All areas that I was willing to draw behaviour management principles from (don't knock it until you've tried it). In short, I had got my plan of action together. It was going to start with a routine, continue with some positive reinforcement and end with a reward. In hindsight, maybe feeding them with Haribo wasn't the ideal method of saying well done (their maths teacher next lesson asked me what on earth I had done to the class), and maybe in my haste to make sure that all of them received a sweet in the interests of equality, maybe just maybe I had let some of the correct answers slide. But I *did* have them eating out of the palm of my hand (literally) for the entirety of the lesson. Although I may have spotted a slight eyebrow raise from their class teacher, she could not argue that I hadn't achieved my personal teaching objective of getting them more engaged for longer periods of the lesson. I'd nailed my reward system.

Until the next lesson, when I did a recap and realised that they had been so hell bent on receiving a sweet that they hadn't retained any of the information that I had painstakingly planned to cover in the last lesson. To top it off, they were not impressed that the Haribo bribery was in fact a one-time offer, as quite frankly my student loan did not stretch to feeding 19 teenage boys for any extended period of time. And now I was behind because I was going to have to spend that lesson redoing the lesson before, as this was a topic sure to come up in the exam.

Fail.

Case study: Anonymous primary teacher

When I took over my ITT lessons, I was given a Year 3 class that had great behaviour, apart from one boy. He really struggled to engage in the mornings but was on a part-time timetable so he missed all of the more fun sessions in the afternoon. I figured out that his teachers had tried everything other than giving him the chance to have a bit of fun in the morning. After a bit of research I found out about start and finish trays. My thought was that, at the start of the lesson for a timed period and as soon as he had finished his workbook allocation for the session, he would be able to get the tray back and play.

I was really impressed with myself that it only took three days for him to engage with it, but also that he was getting quicker and quicker at getting his tasks done. It may have looked like he was spending most of the lesson playing, but every time he presented the work to me it didn't look rushed, so he must just be getting it. And his disruption to the whole class was ebbing, meaning I was getting more teaching done, so win win, right?

Wrong! It took the classroom TA to point out to me that he was playing me... regularly. In my desperation to get him to engage and not disrupt the class, I only asked him to show me the page in his booklet that he had completed, before he was allowed to get his tray that was full of his dinosaur treasures. I was still at the stage of teaching where maybe I wasn't able to take on the amount of information that I can now. Had I developed this skill, I would have been able to take in that it was in fact the same piece of work that he had shown me for the last few days running. You see, he had spotted that I had missed a page of his work, and as there were no ticks on it, and it was a worksheet-esque booklet, he got to day four of showing me the same thing. And here I was, boasting in the staff room that my booklet and tray were working wonders for the boy who refused to engage with his numeracy lessons.

I don't know if that TA took me aside to help me save face as I was telling people, 'He works well for me', or if she did it to save me from the wrath of the class teacher whose lessons I was taking from her to fulfil my teacher training hours, but I do know that I was glad she told me, as I think he would still be holding that scam with me now if he was given half the chance!

My tips to you are:

- Don't be smug and boast if you can get a child to do something that another teacher can't.
- There is always a honeymoon period for a reward.
- Make sure all your marking is up to date and hone your ability to scan work quickly!

It doesn't matter which school of thought you come from regarding behaviour management strategies and techniques, it is highly likely that you will have taken some time to consider your methods for rewarding and sanctioning the behaviour that you experience in your class.

While as a default setting you will find that you adhere to your school's whole-school policy, you should always have your own quality-first techniques in place, as this will give you the ability and stance to escalate undesirable behaviour and solidify wanted actions. I think it is important to have your own systems in place as, if you are always straight away sanctioning to the harshest extent of the law, you run the risk of desensitising your steps of intervention. Also, if that involves getting an external person involved straight away, whether that be a different classroom teacher, a head of department, a head of year or a member of the SLT, you can accidentally send the message that you personally have very little control of the behaviour that you have in your class, resulting in some of the respect that you would like to command being removed from you and passed on to the person who is dealing with the incident. Just think of that teacher who always has pupils sent to their classroom because of their behaviour. I sometimes question whether their behaviour management is perceived as better because of the initial graft that they have put into achieving respect and compliance from all students, meaning that they actually reach a level where their reputation precedes them so their intervention becomes minimal. This is not to say that when the situation warrants it you shouldn't escalate situations. You very much should, but make sure you are choosing the right times and scenarios to play this card as sometimes, once that card has been used, the other steps of intervention are more difficult to employ with certain pupils.

What does the research say about sanctions and rewards?

While I have my own strong and personal views on the usage of sanctions and rewards in the classroom, I thought that it might be nice to share some similarly strong stances from the research to help you determine where you yourself stand, and how you are going to use sanctions and rewards to your advantage.

Rewards

'Of all the rewards given, grades are the most common.' (Seoane and Smink, 1991)

We are an education system of testing. Through all of the key stages, we have a common goal of getting results for our pupils. Even if your particular year group's focus is not on the exams, I would bet that your scheme of work is still leaning towards supporting their eventual outcomes. This means that our pupils often see rewards as the grades that they achieve. Whether it is for them personally, or drilled in at home, the achievement that can be harnessed from their learning alone is not something that should be overlooked, and this will always come from quality-first teaching. In essence, I am saying the first element of reward that they can receive is your delivery of consistently engaging and intellectually progressing content aiding them through their learning journey.

'The presence of intrinsic motivation produces many behaviours that result in school success like sustained interest in tasks, risk-taking, and the conquering of new challenges.' (Adelman and Taylor, 1990; Amabile and Gitomer, 1984; Spaulding, 1992)

Intrinsic motivation is a concept that is reccurring when it comes to studies in rewards and sanctions. Ultimately, we are trying to cultivate a culture where the rewards are more sustainable and more likely to lead to a better result when they come from within the person trying to achieve, rather than from an external factor trying to replicate that emotion and drive.

I would argue that intrinsic motivators occur naturally amongst some pupils. However, for others, there may need to be a period where they are gradually weaned off extrinsic motivators by thorough explanations of self-motivating techniques, cognitive behaviour therapy and outcomes that can lead to that individual being able to find reward from within.

'Teachers can have an easier time dealing with misbehaviour if they try to recognize the motivational basis of misbehaviour.' (Adelman and Taylor, 1990)

This is an interesting concept, but have you ever been in the situation where the pupil gets something from their misbehaviour that can inadvertently be a positive outcome for them? That might be their parents having to come into school, being sent to work in a different space or with someone they deep down want to spend time with, getting more one-to-one interaction or more attention, the class laughing at them (especially if they struggle with making and maintaining friendships), or maybe to the extreme extent, exclusion (resulting in them being able to spend time at home, away from school, where they didn't want to be in the first place, and with the things that they prefer to do like a games console or the internet!). We need to be very mindful of trying to break down the behaviours that are leading to some of the negative behaviours in our classrooms, tailoring our rewards and sanctions to the needs of each child to try and negate the chances that what may seem like a sanction to one is actually a reward to another.

You can get to know the needs of each child by interacting with their previous class teacher. Using the knowledge of what has come before will immediately give you an insight as to what might work for this specific child. Also, having pastoral conversations along these lines or seeking out other key adults in the child's life, including parents, provides a useful starting point to understanding the motivators that they may need.

A child who completes their work with the outcome of being able to demonstrate to themselves how neat their handwriting can be would be seen as intrinsically motivated. One who wrote neatly in the hope that their work would be displayed on the board may be seen as extrinsically motivated. If you provide a treat every time a pupil does something such as enter the classroom quietly, are they actually understanding that the benefits are that you can be calm and ready to start learning, thus losing very little learning time and achieving more time engaging with the task in hand, or are they learning that quiet equals some sort of sugary gelatinous treat? Meaning: are we not then just one step away from being a dog trainer with chicken in their pocket?

Sanctions

While the research has shown that rewards can affect the learning process by undermining a student's intrinsic motivation, does that mean that we should back away from it completely and revert to sanction for improved outcomes?

'The goal of a sanction is to inculcate respect for school rules. Sanction can be consiidered as a regulator of school-life rules and classroom management to help children to learn the human values of respect, obedience and cooperation. The decision to punish, or sanction, a pupil is a cognitive process based on moral judgement.' (Salvano-Pardieu et al., 2009)

This is a pretty intellectual way of saying that it's quite complex to be able to accurately attribute blame, consequence and sanction to a scenario, and sanctions are often based on personal judgement. So, before we sanction, we need to enter into the scenario in the fairest but firmest way possible.

The researchers Allman and Slate (2011) remind us that unwanted behaviours of students in school are not new. Behaviour problems have in fact been reported since the advent of the public school system and teachers have always used a number of sanctions to deal with them. These could be verbal reprimands, after-school detention, in-school suspension, out-of-school suspension, and even fines and corporal punishment (although thankfully that last one has been confined to history in the UK at least). Researchers have expressed concern over several of these methods, including those relating to removing students from the classroom, because it was found that these did not address the behavioural issues and in fact encouraged poor behaviour.

Issuing detentions specifically is a contentious topic. Fabelo et al. (2011) found that detention did not improve academic performance, while Payne (2015) found in a survey of students aged 11 to 16 at a school in England that detentions did not make children behave any better. Students may learn that their bad behaviour may have consequences, but they are not actually learning to behave any better.

One researcher, Holcomb (2016), suggests using a Positive Behaviour Intervention System (PBIS) in place of detention. It aims to encourage and promote positive behaviour and good choices around behaviour. This involves setting expectations, teaching positive behaviours, building relationships, having peer mediators, presenting creative rewards, matching students with mentors, developing behaviour contracts with input from students, teaching social and emotional skills, and working through minor incidents.

The research that I have presented to you here should give you some jumping-off points if you want to look more deeply into the psychology of sanctions and rewards, but in order for us to look at this in relation to your own teaching practice, first you need to understand your own personal values in this area and then you need to see how they align with your school's policy. Use this research to provoke your own thoughts on how you are able to strike the correct balance between carrot and stick. This will come from experience and from trial and error over time, which leads me quite nicely into some plays to assist you.

Plays for the playbook

Trial and error

Some tactics will work and some won't – it's as simple as that! But remember that, although something may not have worked on a certain individual or on a whole class, that is not to say that it is unusable, just that now is not the right time for it to be used. I have surprised myself on more than one occasion by digging something out from the archives and it actually working.

Different ages and different stages

Make sure that the rewards and sanctions that you pick are appropriate for the age and stage you're teaching. Many tactics are fundamentally the same for all age groups but just need some adjustment as pupils grow up. Compare, for example, standing with the lunchtime supervisor at playtime and lunchtime detention. Really they are both the same: after all they amount to the removal of lunchtime freedom in exchange for poor behaviour choices. But making sure that rewards and sanctions fit the age group means that pupils can relate to the behavioural adjustment that you are trying to administer. I will, however, say that no matter the age pupils love stickers. Yes, even sixth formers!

Observe what's around and relevant

By going to see what other staff do, you will add to your arsenal of options when putting together your rewards and sanctions. Borrowing ideas from colleagues, whether in your school, online or from books allows you to keep things fresh, especially if you feel that you have exhausted all of your options. Collaboration can also be the key. Ask other staff members who also work with your pupils whether they've found specific rewards or sanctions that do the trick. This can help you to build more consistency in that child's learning experience and find more areas where they can understand similar if not the same boundaries.

Be consistent

I can never stress this one enough, and if it seems like it's a recurring theme, that's because it is. If you are over-rewarding or over-sanctioning someone, it will be noticed, not just by them but by the class. Inconsistency leaves you with a hole in your practice and can lead to a place where pupils may feel it is OK to question or challenge your decisions. There will always be instances where some pupils may be much further down the sanctions road than others, but take the time to explain: 'Yes [insert pupil name], we will always start each lesson fresh, but this is now the fourth lesson that you are displaying the same behaviours. You clearly aren't learning from this so I'm going to have to try a different approach and unfortunately it looks like you are choosing for this to be escalated more quickly.' Some school policies already support this way of thinking but others do not. Ultimately you need to have in place what is right for your environment but keep it consistent.

> **Reflective space: So... you have a great method to reward and sanction**

We're going to use some bespoke reflection questions in this chapter too. The following questions should help you to go some way towards developing a usable, bespoke reward package for the individual, and also give you the steps towards more effective classroom behaviour reward systems.

1. Who are your most unmotivated pupils? Why are they unmotivated?

_____

_____

_____

_____

2. Is there any further digging that you can do to help with their motivation? What interests them?

_____

_____

_____

_____

3. Are they learning for the reward or themselves? Would the switch to learning for themselves be possible to achieve if you implemented a plan of action?

_____

_____

_____

_____

4. Do we need to train pupils to be intrinsically motivated?

_____

_____

_____

_____

5. Are your expectations clear? How are they reinforced? Verbally or visually (or both)?

_____

_____

_____

_____

6. Are pupils seeking rewards that outweigh the urge to work?

_____

_____

_____

_____

7. Are they trying to negatively get interaction when it could be developed for them to achieve it in a positive way?

_____

_____

_____

_____

8. How regularly do you take time to go over your classroom expectations?

_____

_____

_____

_____

9. How can the reward be the activity in itself?

_____

_____

_____

_____

10. Does one of your stances outweigh the other, i.e. do you believe in the carrot more than the stick or vice versa?

_____

_____

_____

_____

11. What does student motivation look like within your school on a daily basis?

_____

_____

_____

_____

12. Do you have a passion to address this need from a whole-school approach if it is lacking?

_____

_____

_____

_____

Chapter 9

So... you're finding your school's behaviour policy hard to follow

Year 10, last period on a Friday in June, and we're working in the only computer room in the school with no air con. The lads have been running around playing football just ten minutes before and the classroom is that vintage hue of Lynx Africa, body odour and regret (that they are in their ICT lesson and not still trying to achieve 'top bins' outside or smash the ball into an unsuspecting Year 7 or teacher's face). Despite the stench, my classroom of fermenting boys is working silently on task with their blazers off. They are a notoriously difficult bunch, and I had overheard in my first week how I had been given the ultimate graveyard shift having them in that slot. The curse of being the new guy.

I had altered my planning to take this into account, ensuring that all the theory work was done Monday Lesson 1 (another difficult slot but for different reasons as those sleepy boys didn't wake up until after break, but actually I found it an ideal time to get them writing, as the protest side of their brains hadn't woken up either). That left the other graveyard shift to be self-directed practical time, as they had a controlled assessment of 50 hours' input that needed to be completed.

As agreed as a class, if they had achieved enough work throughout the week, I would put the radio on in that Friday slot. It was a great environment, they were focused and the music was on low, the rule being if their volume went louder than the radio or their work rate dropped, the radio would come off. They were so keen to keep it on that they never broke it. The only problem was that there was a school policy that there was no music allowed on during lessons. It wasn't written down anywhere (as I had checked) but it appeared to be an unwritten rule.

This was something that I struggled with because ICT is a very practical subject where a nice buzz can lead to great controlled collaborative work, but also, I'd just left a school where this buzz was the norm. You could go from ICT suite to ICT suite to find the most amazing work going on, but also identify the teacher by the music eking out of the open door: classical, the hits, dubstep (I didn't see how this one helped but the class apparently voted for it!).

I weighed up my options and decided that all would be fine for me to use the music as the benefits far outweighed the negatives and because this classroom was located four floors up and no one ever bothered to visit me.

Wrong wrong wrong.

I discovered this when I joked with the class that I'd never known them so quiet, only to turn around from helping the lad I was with and walk full on into the head. They had gone quiet, because they, like I, was aware of the unwritten 'no music' rule. They were also probably very confused about who would get into trouble with this strict head. If I was going down, were they going down with me? I don't know how long she had been there, but it was long enough for her to extend to me a formal invitation to her office after school to discuss why I felt I was above the behaviour management policy.

Great first impression.

In all truth, I wasn't above the policy, but it was a quick lesson in my realising that maybe this wasn't the right school for me after all. I'd like to say that I abided by the school's no music policy, but instead, we all got adept at it being on low and whoever was nearest switching it off if anyone approached. My head of department laughed and told me repeatedly that he didn't care for that archaic rule either. I stayed long enough with that school for me to finish teaching that year group. My class went on to get the highest average GCSE grades that year and I reckon it was all down to the relaxed musical lessons! But it wasn't the place for me. I knew I didn't align with their values, so it was me who had to find a school where I did.

It is very important not only to work alongside your school, but also to implement your own zone of strategy: a behaviour management policy for your classroom. I now have the pleasure of inviting Sarah Mullin, author of *What I Wish They'd Taught Me on My PGCE*, and Ross Morrison McGill of @TeacherToolkit to come in and provide some areas of thought and support. First up, Sarah tells us more about the benefits and importance of a whole-school behaviour management policy and how she developed an effective policy as an assistant headteacher in a secondary school.

Case study: Sarah Mullin, deputy headteacher

So... you think children can't design their own behaviour policy?

Pupil behaviour and learning outcomes are inextricably linked. According to research from the Education Endowment Foundation (EEF; 2019), a school's approach to behaviour management is likely to be most effective when considered in conjunction with staff, pupils and parents. On average, children with higher levels of school wellbeing have higher levels of academic achievement and are more engaged in school, both concurrently and in later years. Furthermore, students' school experience 'remains one of the most insightful indicators' of their future life outcomes (Bennett, 2017). When I first took responsibility for pastoral care as an assistant headteacher at an 11–18 secondary school, I was keen to implement a clear and consistent behaviour policy that would promote positive behaviour across the school.

Pupil behaviour is regularly cited as impacting on the atmosphere in classrooms, influencing the educational progress children and young people make; I firmly believe that pupils must feel happy, safe and supported in their environment in order to thrive. My first task was to explore the perceptions and experiences of pupils, parents, staff and governors. Through the use of anonymous questionnaires and small focus groups, it was clear that pupils felt that behaviour management was not always consistent, with sanctions varying depending on the teacher issuing them. Pupils felt that the sanctions given across the school were not always in line with the behaviour issue and that there was not enough focus on praising those who behaved positively. My aim was to design a behaviour policy in collaboration with staff, pupils and parents in order to improve pupil perception of behaviour management at the school. I was keen to enhance pupil engagement, ensuring that pupils felt that their voices were being heard, improving standards so that pupils felt that they were being treated fairly and consistently at all times.

Bennett (2017) suggests that school leaders must aim for the highest possible behaviour standards, implementing and proactively monitoring a clear policy which is used consistently by all members of the school community. As a passionate school leader determined to drive positive change to ensure the highest standards of behaviour at the school, I carefully devised an action plan that responded to the voices of pupils, staff and parents. By engaging all members of the school community in the process, I was able to understand their concerns, critically reflecting on the existing sanction and reward systems and collaboratively producing a clear policy which could be applied fairly and consistently by all staff at all times. By listening to the views of pupils and by taking on board their suggestions for a uniform behaviour system, I believed that pupils would feel that their voices were being heard; that they would appreciate that they were valued and feel that they were responsible for making positive changes to the school community. To inspire the trust and respect of all those involved in my initiative, it was important for me to lead ethically and authentically, letting my passion shine through and showing that I was acting in the best interests of all stakeholders at all times. I truly believed that, although it would be hard work initially, the impact of a new collaborative policy would benefit everybody involved. I stayed true to my core values and beliefs throughout the process, especially when I encountered challenges along the way.

Theorists such as Piaget (1959) and Vygotsky (1978) argue that children should be actively involved in their own learning. By introducing a new system which pupils helped to design in collaboration with their teachers, I believed that they would benefit from a consistent approach to issuing sanctions and rewards across the school by all teachers at all times. We classified types of behaviour into a 'traffic light system'. We divided them clearly into yellow, amber and red categories, depending on the severity or frequency of the incident, to ensure that the language we were using to describe behaviour was consistent across the school. In addition, a clear system for issuing sanctions and rewards was established through the introduction of this 'traffic light system'. The introduction of the behaviour improvement policy was launched in my first term at the school and it was well received by staff, pupils, parents and governors. In our subsequent inspection, the lead reporting inspector praised the improved policy, commenting, 'Pupils are proud of their school... they understand the school's system of rewards and sanctions and value the contribution this makes to high standards of behaviour in school.'

The new behaviour system improved behaviour management at the school and the number of children being issued with more serious sanctions, such as isolations, suspensions and exclusions, reduced dramatically in the years after its implementation. Feedback from pupils and their parents showed that they felt they were being treated fairly and consistently, and furthermore, pupils showed understanding that for every action there is a reaction, preparing them for life after school as a law-abiding citizen.

So, if you are thinking about how to build positive relationships in your classroom, your department or your school, why not try asking your pupils to help design their own sanction and reward systems? The results may pleasantly surprise you.

Sarah Mullin is a deputy headteacher from the West Midlands. She is currently completing her professional doctorate in education and she is renowned for delivering CPD to student teachers and early career teachers across the UK and internationally. Sarah also coaches women aspiring to school leadership. She is the author of the number one bestselling book What They Didn't Teach Me on My PGCE *and she is the founder of #EduTeacherTips, a YouTube channel for teachers by teachers. Sarah received the 'Contribution to Education of the Year' award in 2019 and she has recently been named a 'Rising Star in Education and Academia'. She has previously been named as an 'Inspirational Woman' and has been shortlisted as a finalist in the categories of Headteacher of the Year, Teacher of the Year and a Positive Role Model (Gender) by the National Diversity Awards.*

Case study: Ross Morrison McGill, @TeacherToolkit

Recently, I visited a school to observe a number of lessons. As one would expect, walking a school's corridors gives me a sense of school ethos, vision and day-to-day expectations. This is largely what inspectors do when they visit your school. They make subjective decisions based on classroom and corridor conversations. Thankfully, I am conscious of bias and poor proxies for learning, in other words, things easily observed but that tell us nothing about learning, so I do what I can to ensure no judgements or spurious claims about effectiveness are made. With this in mind, I arrived with the pupils to class and witnessed the behaviour policy translated, used and put into action from the moment students arrived. It was heartwarming.

However, the corridors offered the typical chaos one would expect when hundreds of pupils are herded into confined spaces – I wish architects of school buildings would consider the use of school corridors more thoughtfully – with some pupils moving along in a hurry or others dawdling at a lethargic pace. These patterns of movement happen in every school. When you squeeze pupils into communal spaces, ring a bell and expect them to reach their destination before the time runs out (resulting in detention), you would be forgiven for thinking, 'Why is there so much loud banging and shouting between lesson changeover?'

Policy in practice

As pupils arrived, they walked to their classroom desk positions. Pupils took off their jackets and remained standing behind their chairs. Each pupil stood at their chair until the teacher 'chose' to start the lesson. Until this happened, the teacher was standing at the door, meeting and greeting each pupil – offering some instruction. The teacher was following the behaviour policy to the letter. So were the pupils. The lesson started calmly and there was zero disruption. Yet, at a deeper level, although I can understand the value of doing such a thing, I started to ask myself the following questions seven to ten minutes into the lesson as the teacher continued to stand at the door, whilst some pupils continued to stand behind their chairs waiting for the others in the class to arrive:

1. Does the behaviour policy support learning?
2. What could pupils be doing instead of just standing behind chairs?
3. If you were a pupil, would it be easier to arrive last to the lesson so it starts when you arrive?
4. What sanctions could be imposed on pupils if the policy insists that pupils must stand and they don't do it?
5. What value does standing behind a chair at the start of every lesson have on learning?

6. What happens in classrooms where teachers do not use the policy?
7. What does this policy look like in different classrooms, e.g. Year 1, Year 11 and sixth form? Design technology or maths?
8. Is there any research evidence to suggest this approach works when compared to:
   ◦ lining up outside
   ◦ starting the lesson as soon as pupils arrive
   ◦ issuing sanctions for those who are late beyond an agreed transition time?

Tweaking teaching and learning

I am not against schools doing this. In fact, I think it's a great idea to help support whole-school expectations, yet valuable learning time is lost if a potentially good idea lacks refinement or sets inexperienced teachers up to fail. A simple second warning bell to indicate that movement between classrooms has now ended and that the next lesson has started is a quick fix. This warning bell symbolises to pupils and teachers a clear division between leaving, arrival and starting the next class.

Alternatively, a teacher could provide students with an activity to do (on arrival) whilst on their feet. This would help frame the lesson ahead, but what impact it has while the teacher manages pupils arriving at the door is a real challenge. Do I attend to my classroom entrance, or do I attend to those pupils who have arrived on time who want to get on with the learning?

Ross Morrison McGill is the founder and CEO of @TeacherToolkit. He is an experienced teacher and school leader with a career history spanning over 25 years in state schools across London. He is also an award-winning author and blogger.

It's clear from Ross's case study that most school behaviour policies will have pros and cons. Often when a new head enters a school, the first thing they will look at is behaviour, as with good behaviour comes the ability to learn in a safe and nurturing environment, so everything else should fall into place if this is right. Different schools have different stances, and there's nothing wrong with any of them as long as they are working to support learning. The only thing that I struggle with is when a school deems that their way is the perfect way and everyone should follow. In my humble opinion, it is very difficult to have one uniform approach to behaviour regardless of setting, as the issues that you may find in an inner-city school will change vastly from those that you may find in a rural school or those that you may find in a school based in an area of wealth. I have worked in all three, and I wouldn't say that any of their behaviour issues were less than the other. In some cases, they just weren't comparable and were very much worlds apart.

The balance of a good system can be difficult to achieve, and the school will need to decide which stakeholders are important to them. It might usually remain unsaid, but I'm going to ask the question: who is the policy for? Is it for the pupils, the parents, the teachers, the community, the league tables or even Ofsted?! As someone who visits different schools regularly, I know that you can usually tell.

Is this the right school for you?

So, one of the main considerations from these thought processes on a school's policy mainly realigns to: is it the right school for you? Aligning your principles and ethos so that you can fit in well with a school starts way before you start working there. Even before you cross the threshold, on application to a school, you have the ability to storm their virtual space. Looking at their website and downloading their prospectus will straight away set out their intent. Even the covering letter or headteacher's address attached to the job application can highlight the way that school thinks and aims to work. If you still have a burning desire to be a part of the school once you've done your research, you can get a feel for your potential new establishment just from walking around a) at lesson changeover and b) during lesson time. Are the pupils behaving because it's natural to them, or are they behaving because they've spotted a particular member of staff they know will follow through on a sanction, only to act completely differently when they see the next teacher because they are a walkover?

Are the pupils invested in the system? Do they see the benefits that are in it for them? Or are there nothing but benefits, reward after reward with no intrinsic desire to do the right thing? Or the flip side, is it pure stick with no carrot, losing the child-centred approach? Let us not forget that ultimately we are working with children who are trying to find their way in the world and figure out who they are, and are kind of wired to find the boundaries and try and push up against them.

Not only are the pupils invested, but are the staff invested? Do they use that policy to the letter of the law with no leeway, sometimes rendering it overused and ineffective because they have no personal management skills to lean upon? Or are they a dog leg, refusing to comply in any way, shape or form, with no recording of incidents, no follow-through and no consequence? (In case you don't know the expression, a dog leg is when, in certain sports like rugby, you are meant to be in a defensive line in the same formation and one person is out of sync, allowing the opposition to spot that weakness and run through. The dog leg is created by someone not being on the same page and therefore creating a weak spot.) Although these are two extremes of attitudes towards behaviour management, they are attitudes that can exist, and attitudes that can make it even more difficult for you to be able to work effectively.

Your personal ethos is something that you need to consider when applying to become a part of an establishment, and nowadays this is not just the physical school that you are a part of, but it also extends to the local authority (LA) or multi-academy trust (MAT) that your school umbrellas underneath, because whatever it is, you need to be a part of that team. Some MATs run in such a way that they have overarching values but let the individual school run as their own entity. Others have blanket expectations for all, so additional research on a school's MAT expectations may be needed in order for you to make an informed decision.

Whatever the school ethos, it really is your responsibility to try and figure it out before you say yes to taking on a role with them. Whether you agree or disagree, if there is a dog leg to the approach of their policies, for right or for wrong, it will not work. If within your classroom, you are the one who is doing your version of what you see fit with no regard to the whole-school approach, you are going to struggle, feel resentment and maybe even have feelings of resentment towards you. Especially from a member of staff who does follow the policy but is constantly hearing, 'Well, Mr Harper says it's fine.' We all know that teacher, people. Don't be that teacher.

I have seen far too many excellent teachers leave the profession, not because they couldn't do the job, but because the school and themselves were not the right fit. I have seen staff go on to action plans and feel like they are useless, only to move school and thrive, flourish and progress. Even I have been at a school that made me think that I had lost my touch with teaching when in fact I had the right touch in the wrong school.

Plays for the playbook

For this section of the playbook, I felt that it would be really useful to gain some additional insight and expertise from an educator who has been in the business even longer than me, who has a lot of experience in his career and who is a prolonged example of someone who takes his time to help others via his own books and blogs. Ross's behaviour script will give you some clear strategic steps to work through whilst you still might be in the infancy of your career and may need clear prompts before it all becomes second nature (which it will one day).

Seven-step behaviour script
(by Ross Morrison McGill, @TeacherToolkit)

Below I have outlined how teachers can build a better behaviour ethos and how teachers can manage behaviour more effectively in their conversations with students. It is essential to develop a script which can become routine and then adapt it to a variety of scenarios in your classroom.

1. Have a pep talk

Getting behaviour right is a complex process. Approach any situation calmly. Get to the root of the problem and quash all low-level disruption. It is essential that all teachers become excellent at classroom management as well as being at the forefront of their subject knowledge.

2. Verbal warning

Aim to have a quiet conversation with the student. This avoids losing face for the student, and on your part, ensures other students cannot intervene with comments or reactions. If the student refuses to come with you – even if it is just five to ten metres away – have the chat later.

3. Issue a sanction in the classroom

Approach the conversation in a non-threatening position, adopting a neutral body position where the student's vantage point is facing away from peers.

4. Have a 30-second catch-up

You need to communicate *what* has happened and that the student will have an opportunity to respond at the end. Explain what the behaviour is. Where you need help, seek training for high-level incidents and be proactive in analysing behaviour trends.

5. Ask the pupil to stay behind

Provide the student with a reason *why* you have intervened and have a pep talk with them. At this point refer to two or three keywords (and no more) from the school's behaviour policy. The secret is to establish with your students the difference between being fair and equal.

6. Set an imposition

Explain *how* the student could make this better. The most effective strategy I have found to work consistently is to show how (through explanation and modelling) the behaviour will be perceived by other students, other teachers, visitors, and most of all their family. Involving contact at home is essential for positive and negative episodes, so do make sure you follow up with both, not just the negatives.

7. Involve a second adult

Finish by ending the pep talk with a question. Where relevant, ask the student if they would like *you* to feel proud of them. Every single time I have asked this question to a child, their response has always been a 'yes'. Who wouldn't want admiration? Most importantly keep your message simple. Focus on the primary behaviour.

*

Whether stage 1 ends the behaviour at that point or you need to escalate the sanctions up to stage 7 where a second adult is required will depend on countless scenarios. Context is key.

Consistency is fundamental to what you do as a teacher, whether you are in your first year of the classroom or your 30th. Once you have got to know your students well, have developed a secure overview and a strong set of relationships, this mutual respect can secure silence at the drop of a hat.

Reproduced with kind permission from Ross Morrison McGill,
@TeacherToolkit.

Reflective space: So... you're finding your school's behaviour policy hard to follow

While you may feel that the answer to being at odds with your school's behaviour policy is to find a new setting where your ideals match with those of the school, there are some options before you hand in your notice and move on. Think about engaging with any behaviour steering groups that may be in place in your school. If they don't exist, talk to your SLT about your interest in having an input on the policies and behaviour management actions should the opportunity ever arise.

Get involved with the school council and hear the pupil voice around issues of behaviour. See where you can have a valid input at a pupil level and support them by bringing their ideas to senior leaders. Consider school governance. As a teacher governor, you will be able to have an input on the running of the school, including behaviour policies, what's working, what isn't and more importantly how it can be improved.

But for now, let us think back to a moment when you felt at odds with your school's behaviour management policy. What happened and what could you take away from that experience to help next time? Write some notes in response to the following questions to shape your thought processes.

1. What happened?

_____

_____

_____

_____

2. Was this experience personal?

_____

_____

_____

_____

3. How did the incident make you feel?

_____

_____

_____

_____

4. Is there a repeat offender involved in the situation?

_____

_____

_____

_____

5. Were there any catalysts or red flags to the incident?

_____

_____

_____

_____

6. Have you decided to take any additional steps (e.g. call home, detention, involving another member of staff)?

_____

_____

_____

_____

7. Do you feel like leaving the classroom? Why?

_____

_____

_____

_____

8. What's one thing that you would do differently if the same situation were to arise?

_____

_____

_____

_____

Chapter 10

So... you think ladies can't manage behaviour as well as men

Now this chapter is a really interesting concept to me. As you can tell by the fact that I'm writing this book, behaviour management is a real passion of mine and I feel my expertise has been enhanced by being a woman rather than hampered. However, what is interesting as you scour the literature surrounding the concepts, teachings, preaching and practice of behaviour management, it seems to be a male-dominated area. If you take a quick look at the demographic of school leaders, with more men in senior positions of authority than in classroom-teaching roles, it perhaps seems, on the surface, that behaviour management lends itself towards being a more male-orientated task. But does this mean then that men are better at managing pupil behaviour?

In short, the answer is no. One of the best managers of behaviour I have ever come across was an absolute pocket rocket who was also female. You could barely see her above the desk, but my God could you feel her presence as soon as you entered her classroom. While I believe that males can possess some natural dominance features that may contribute towards having more control of a class (stature, voice pitch, societal assumptions and norms), I do not believe that any of these things cannot be bottled, replicated and used to your advantage regardless of your gender.

I have wondered whether there have been any studies or significant findings in the research around possible differences between female and male classroom and corridor control, or whether it is merely a perception and stereotype. It will always be an interesting fact to me that a number of studies have found that imposter syndrome or imposter feeling is more prevalent in females than males, and even more so in young people. Interestingly, I feel that this affects a huge number of the NQTs who enter the classroom to teach. Teaching is a female-dominated environment, although this is still not fully reflected in school leadership. This can lead to the question of how women can feel adequately empowered and capable if they are struggling and they find there are very few role models out there available to demonstrate how to behaviour-manage by someone who is similar to them.

I feel that this chapter could be a whole book in itself, and who knows, maybe I will write it one day, but in the meantime, ladies, you can take comfort from the fact that this chapter is here for you, even if only for you to say, oh yes, this is me. But also for the guys out there, this is a great opportunity for you to listen to some of the inadvertent factors that may affect your female colleagues and think twice before you utter, 'Oh well, they behave for me', and wonder why the recipient of those words has launched their coffee mug across the staff room and into the back of your head – because although they may behave for you, it may not be for all the reasons that you think.

It is also great if you are (or ever become) a leader in charge of monitoring pupil behaviour, and you have found a hotspot where behaviour isn't what you would expect. Is there a bigger job of looking at the attitudes of the pupils in your school in regard to how they respect their female teachers compared to their male counterparts? All questions that are valid for perusal at your leisure.

What *does* the research say?

Findings in various studies reveal that there is no significant difference between male and female teachers in terms of judging behaviours. Both male and female teachers have a general tendency to judge the disruptive students in the same way (Salvano-Pardieu et al., 2009). However, studies have identified links between classroom management style and gender. Martin, Yin and Mayall (2007), for example, reveal that there is a significant difference between classroom management approaches of female and male teachers. In their study, they found newly graduated teachers' and male teachers' classroom management approaches had a tendency to be more intrusive, directing and controlling.

It's an intriguing concept to think that male teachers are deemed as more 'intrusive', and it got me thinking about whether this was actually the case, as surely it is down to the perception of those on the receiving and observing end. It is much easier to be deemed 'intrusive' and 'controlling' if you have a classroom presence that immediately allows you to dictate the mood from your position in the classroom. I cannot help but think back to a time when I was at school and an English teacher struggled to get our class to be quiet, mainly, in hindsight, because we couldn't hear her high-pitched, soft-spoken voice over our din, and her response was to take off her shoe and bang it on the desk. The only message she sent to us that afternoon was that if we were loud enough, we might possibly have the ability to tip her over the edge, meaning we wouldn't have to participate in her lesson. It didn't evoke any type of respect or trigger anything in our brains that associated it with controlling our behaviour. Whereas a male member of staff may just have to clear his deep, baritone voice and the silence that ensues is enough to hear a pin drop.

This area isn't just a thought-provoker for me, as our case study teachers for this chapter, Elizabeth and Genevieve, can attest to.

Case study: Elizabeth Swan, experienced school leader

Standing in front of the class of Year 8s, rivulets of sweat poured down the back of my neck. Beads of spit were highlighted by the beam of light from the overhead projector as I tried to make myself heard over the flightpath from Heathrow and the increasing voices of dissent from pre-teens uninterested in learning how to conjugate German modal verbs. The previous night I had spent three hours planning this lesson, handcrafting multi-sensory resources, shying away from the textbook for fear of accusations of a lack of creativity. I'd arrived at school before 7.15 am to spend an hour making 'kinaesthetic' matching activities and worksheets for the lesson. The love and care I had poured into the resources and planning were not reflected in the pupils' engagement or learning at this moment. Hot, overwhelmed and confused. Was this the pupils or the teacher?

As a teacher who had excelled at behaviour management throughout her teacher training, I did not want the pupils to sense my vulnerability. The noise was escalating in the room and pupils could sense that I was struggling to regain control of the situation. I was fearful that my head of department next door would hear the noise and think I was unable to manage behaviour. Pupils began to heckle me, like drunks at a comedy night. The heat flooded my face and I was no longer able to see the lesson plan, which I had meticulously scripted the previous night. As MFL teachers, we were trained throughout our PGCE to script behaviour management instructions in the target language in the lesson plan, a supportive strategy until you're unable to find your lesson plan under a mountain of paper-sorting activities. As I rummaged on my desk for my script, the pupils realised that I was distracted. I had lost control of behaviour. My desire to control everything in the lesson by micro-managing had ultimately led to losing control. While the pupils were fully aware of my loss of control, I was still oblivious and trying to instil order.

At this point, pupils were not only shouting across the room, but some pupils were now launching missiles across the room and walking around freely – it was anarchy! Identifying who I believed to be the kingpin, I called him to the front of the room and decided to make an example of him – a sacrificial lamb so that the pupils would then realise I was boss. Protesting his innocence as he came to the front, the other pupils shouting messages of support for him, I summoned up my full height, shoulders back, deep breath and decided I needed to really instil some proper discipline in the pupil and his classmates. As I began my tirade the class dropped silent. I froze and my cheeks flushed. As I had begun to shout, all of the stress from the situation had relaxed out of my body in one ginormous fart. Loud enough to eclipse even the noise from the Heathrow flightpath.

My top tips for behaviour management are:

1. **Own your space:** Your classroom is your space. Welcome the pupils into your space each lesson, with your set routines, set boundaries and set expectations. Know your school's policies and protocols inside out and apply them consistently. Work on a 3:1 ratio with praise : discipline, which is shared with home.
2. **When you lose it, you've lost it:** If you shout, you've lost control of the situation. Take a deep breath in through your nose for four, hold for five and breathe out for six. Speak clearly and calmly. You only

need to raise your voice if a child is in danger, or to be heard at the back of a hall in an assembly.

3. **Find your voice:** I went to drama school from an early age and learnt about how to use voice and how to adopt characters. Stand tall, shoulders back, breathe deeply. Research tips for voice projection to avoid your voice sounding 'shrill'.

4. **Relationships:** Use corridor conversations to call pupils by name and catch up about their football team or favourite band. Remember to keep boundaries tight: pupils need a trusted adult, not a best friend. Allow negative behaviour to 'boing flip' off your deflector shield; don't take it personally.

5. **Kindness:** If you've exhausted all the behaviour strategies in your arsenal, try kindness. What would be the kindest thing you could do right now?

Elizabeth Swan has 12 years' experience and has senior leadership expertise in secondary mainstream schools as an assistant headteacher (inclusion, SENDCo, DSL) and deputy headteacher (pastoral, SENDCo, DSL) and later headteacher of a school for pupils with highly complex social, emotional and mental health needs. It has been 11 years since her NQT year.

We all love a mortifying classroom experience, as it will make us feel better about our own experiences and personal shortcomings. Although I laughed heartily (and I hope you did too), there is so much that we can take from this experience and learn from. The tips from Elizabeth really hone in on some of the skills and techniques we need to perfect to get to a place of control in the classroom.

Case study: Genevieve Bent, associate assistant headteacher

When I started my training year, I looked young. Sixth-former young. I started my first placement at a tough Catholic school where children did not have the best behaviour but it was clear they wanted to learn. I remember my first time entering the staff room and another member of staff blocked me from entering; she told me, 'It's for staff only.' When I had explained, I overheard another member of staff saying, 'That's a teacher?! Good luck.' I was embarrassed and started to wonder if I had made a mistake going into teaching. Would the kids listen to me? Would they want to learn from me? And would I be able to manage behaviour?

I watched my (then) mentor teach the classes that I would soon be taking over: how did she engage them? Were they interested? Did they listen? I would try to take as many tips down as I could. When I started teaching, however, I realised I didn't need to be like her (or any other teacher I'd seen) and I could just be me. The kids took me seriously from the beginning; something about my stern demeanour but friendly manner encouraged the students to listen to and learn from me. I was told by my mentors that I had an authoritative manner and presence; a warm but strict manner and the determination to follow through with my words. This did not mean it was easy. In fact, I often had colleagues undermine my hard efforts in managing behaviour by telling me, 'Oh but you'll be OK. The boys will just be googly-eyed and listen to you', when in fact it was the complete opposite, at first. Boys wanted to constantly outdo each other with poor behaviour around me, and it was only through my steely determination and my unwavering attention and care for them that I was able to 'manage the behaviour' of my students.

After a couple of months, I remember walking out into the corridor and seeing a group of Year 11 boys play-fighting, instead of going to their lessons. As I walked over to bellow at them, they broke apart and I heard one of them walk off and say, 'Nahhhhh, Miss Bent got me two Saturday detentions, not even worth it.' It made my day at the time and still makes me laugh when I think of it. But every day was a new day, and as a teacher in the school, you had to work continuously hard trying to manage behaviour… female or not. Fast forward a few years and I've become a member of staff who can walk into a room, look around and silently request (or not so in some cases) the silence and attention of students when necessary. I continuously aim to be the teacher students choose to listen to and respect but also the one who listens to and respects the students, and 'good' behaviour management means you work towards doing both and maintaining the balance. And that goes for some of my colleagues who are also female and extremely strong in behaviour management. And they say women can't handle behaviour!

Genevieve Bent is an associate assistant headteacher, leading sixth form and science.

Never let anyone undermine your ability to manage behaviour based on looks and gender. As proven here by Genevieve, it is very much your resolve and determination, your consistency and passion, that will make the difference, but most importantly it is you. You who is behind the achievement, you who is behind the reflection and adjustments, you who is behind the environment that you design, create and promote. And you get to take ownership of this and be proud in this knowledge.

What can have an impact on females in the classroom?

It's really important that we discuss this area, regardless of the gender that we are. When we think about behaviour, we must feel comfortable enough to put all potential factors on the table for discussion, analysis and action planning. As we can see from the discussions and case studies above, some may see being female as having a negative impact on behaviour in the classroom. I am really pleased that this narrative is not at all supported in this book but in fact countered by the number of solid female voices we have offering not just anecdotes but also tips on how to improve and move forward. However, it is worth taking a look at some factors that may specifically affect women in the classroom.

Absences from the classroom

There are times in a woman's career that may be affected by absences in the classroom. One such example is if we have children. Anecdotes often refer to the same familiar narrative that when a man goes off and starts a family he is seen as being more responsible, more worthy of promotion and even more sympathised towards if his children are having a diverse effect on his working life, whereas a woman can be seen as not as dedicated as she once was, easier to overlook for a promotion and disorganised.

Also, a gap of time away from the classroom can take away confidence and belief in one's ability. This is something that should never happen but unfortunately can. When you return from a hiatus from the classroom, do not be afraid to ask if you can have a structured return, involving things such as observing your classes with other staff, support with lesson-planning to help you catch up with any curriculum changes, and above all, having a support network that you are able to go to for help without judgement or repercussions.

Norms and assumptions at home

Sometimes your behaviour-management ability could be undermined by the gender norms that exist within the households of the pupils you work with. It can be important for you to recognise this and gain support from their home. Unfortunately, you may come across situations where, no matter what you do, pupils are unable to provide you with the respect that you deserve because of this. This means that you may have to put in some extra work to help them understand about equality. There are plenty of formal opportunities for this in PSHE and citizenship lessons but more informally you could try to engage them in topics that are relevant in the press. There are also brilliant picture games for challenging cultural norms with younger children, for example, a game of snap where you match up pictures of people doing the same job, regardless of gender – so you'd match up a female plumber and a male plumber. Putting in the additional time may seem like an exercise that is beyond your lesson-planning expectations or responsibility, but everything we do within our schools is part of the learning experience and is important to help young people to be able to function well and be supportive in society.

School culture – who leads in the school?

If a leadership team is all the same, not only does it limit a diverse thought process, but it can also send out silent modelling lessons to the pupils you work with. So, if you feel that you're up to a more senior role, don't be put off and apply. Women occupying leadership positions may inspire the next generation of female leaders, but can also send a message that authority and leadership come in many different shapes, sizes, appearances and genders.

Stature and build

Can a stocky six foot three male command a learning environment better than a five foot three female? I would always argue that it 100 per cent depends on the individual who is commanding the space. However, it is important to acknowledge that there is potential for unconscious bias and internalised misogyny which may mean behaviour is better with a more physically dominant presence in the room. Nonetheless, this doesn't mean that you cannot recreate ways to develop an artificial presence, whatever your build.

The way that you circulate a room and command your space and the way that you carry yourself will all make a difference. You can make yourself 'big' just by taking a deep breath, pulling your shoulders back and lifting your chin. You can make your presence felt by the projection of your voice. This doesn't mean shouting, but actually controlling the volume as it leaves your stomach to make sure that it can reach the back of the room. You can make your presence felt by recognising the pitch and tone that accompany your voice. Sometimes, when females raise their voices, the result can be a pitchy noise that can feel like it is more grating than effecting. Taking the conscious decision to try and put some bass in your voice can make sure that the message that you are sending over is not lost in delivery.

Plays for the playbook

We're going to take a reflective approach to the plays for this section of the playbook. This could be from your perspective as a woman or it could be as a man looking at behaviour from a female perspective. Perhaps you could think about something you have witnessed or about how you could be supportive in a particular scenario. Either way, I want you to really dig deep on this one. The incident you recall may not be a situation that you thought was related to gender at the time, but if you think about it more deeply, maybe it was.

How quickly are you able to identify when you are starting to lose control of the class?

And what tactics have you put in place for that horror moment when the train does come off the tracks?

Are you in a supportive department or are you living in fear of what others think of your teaching and control?

As leaders, we have all been there when we can hear anarchy coming from a classroom, and when we poke our heads around the door, nothing fills us with greater relief than when we can see that the teacher does in fact have this and it was just a particularly rowdy part of a practical or lively discussion that we have walked in on. It's clear that learning is going on and there's nothing you need from us, so off you go. But most leaders have also been there when we look around that door and we have to compute the horror. As a teacher, there is nothing more demoralising than another teacher disciplining your class, right? Wrong! If it is done in the right way, it can be a very supportive tool, and probably something that teachers in their formative years may see (maybe more often than they would like!). A COF (or change of face) is a very valid and legitimate behaviour management technique. In fact, I would say, as long as not used with too much regularity, there is no harm in requesting one before the leader feels the need to present you with one.

It is also important for the person who is handing out a COF to remember that they are coming in to support. It should not then be used against the teacher at a later stage. It should be completely supportive and followed up with further ways that they can be supported in the future. This will stop any feelings of embarrassment, being 'less than' or not wanting to ask for help in the future.

Does your appearance have an impact on how you control your class?

During the research for this book, I was overwhelmed with how many horror stories came back of advice to female teachers being linked mainly to their appearance. Ideas such as power dressing, wearing red lipstick and always wearing heels. This blew my mind, but I would like to tell you this: if you want to power dress and wear make-up and heels to work, wear them because that is what you want to do. Do not do this because you feel that this will get you some automatic behaviour management points. I can understand that using elements of this method may provide you with confidence (if this is your thing and this is how you find your confidence), but I cannot help but imagine if similar advice was given to male staff (for example, always wear a fitted suit with a red tie and try to get shoe lifts), it would be greeted with complete incredulousness. So, all I will say here is: do whatever you need to do to feel confident, but do not think that your appearance is an important feature in managing a classroom. It simply is not... unless you're having a wardrobe malfunction that will cause classroom hysteria, but who would do that, eh?!

Can the subject you teach have an impact?

There are definitely more female-dominated subjects (and even key stages). But even if this is the case, do not let it have an impact on what you choose to do! I stand by my earlier stance that one of the best members of staff I saw control behaviour was a short female, and she was in turn backed up by one of the most formidable heads of department in the school, who also happened to be female. If the correct structures are in place, it shouldn't matter which subject or key stage you are in, but if they are not, seek out ways to make them better, such as working with the SLT and middle leaders to find best-practice departments within the school and bring some of their tactics back to your department.

> **Reflective space: So... you think ladies can't manage behaviour as well as men**

Has there been a time when you believe your gender has impacted your classroom management? If so, reflect on it below.

1. What happened?

_____

_____

_____

_____

2. Was this experience personal?

_____

_____

_____

_____

3. How did the incident make you feel?

_____

_____

_____

_____

4. Is there a repeat offender involved in the situation?

_____

_____

_____

_____

5. Were there any catalysts or red flags to the incident?

_____

_____

_____

_____

6. Have you decided to take any additional steps (e.g. call home, detention, involving another member of staff)?

_____

_____

_____

_____

7. Do you feel like leaving the classroom? Why?

_____

_____

_____

_____

8. What's one thing that you would do differently if the same situation were to arise?

_____

_____

_____

_____

Chapter 11

So... it all went tits up on a school trip

There are few things more sweat-inducing than realising that you are in charge of pupils in public. No matter their age, they will manage to find their own specific ways of throwing spanners in the works that you never even thought of. The reason why behaviour management on a trip is so different to dealing with behaviour in a school setting is exactly that: the school setting has now gone. A lot of the constants that you don't need to deal with on a day-to-day basis could now be the reason why having control becomes a bit more complicated.

You're never usually in charge of how your pupils get to school, the food they eat throughout the day or even the clothes they wear, whereas on a school trip, particularly residentials, you suddenly need to make sure the 30-plus children are able to travel to their learning destination without accidents or travel sickness, with appropriate bus conversation (if you achieve this on a secondary trip, please could you send me the magic formula?!), all whilst they are sneaking E-numbers into their system at such a rate that the only way for them to receive the rush any faster would be for them to take the sugar intravenously via a drip. Because nothing says school trip like sugary gelatinous goodness. This, combined with the hyped adrenaline that comes with being out of class and the comfortable nature of being in their own clothes, means that there's potential in the air that 'Today, anything could go.'

Evidence generally suggests that such trips can have a positive impact on the learning of facts and concepts, but 'it is important to consider ways of maximizing these outcomes by focusing on field trip designs that make best use of the unique learning opportunities of specific field trip destinations' (DeWitt and Storksdieck, 2008). As well as curriculum-learning opportunities, school trips are a great way to work on positive social outcomes. While there are many possible positive outcomes to a school trip, quite often they are not able to be done at the regularity that we would (maybe) like to do them due to numerous external factors, such as cost, staffing and time constraints.

However, after months (or for a substantial residential trip, years) of planning, when the day rocks up for that trip, you will have no doubt covered all the bases and be more than prepared for every eventuality that will be thrown your way, right? Well, I don't think that this chapter could exist if that were the case. If you know any teacher who has been on a school trip, you'll be hard pressed to find one who hasn't been faced with a moment that, at the time, felt like the end of the world or worse, their career, but that they now look back on with hilarity and fondness – and that is probably their number one pub anecdote (although not to be repeated if there are any authorities in earshot).

I am no different to this. I have my fair share of anecdotes that I could reel off under this topic. However, my moment of school trip horror which I'd like to share with you decided not to take place on a cold, dreary day at a local castle, but instead in New York, in their infamous subway system.

I don't know what was more terrifying about this trip: the incident in question or the fact that at 24, I barely felt qualified to look after my own passport and ESTA, let alone the ten 15-year-olds who had been assigned directly to me as their trip leader, out of a total of 50 15–16-year-olds who would be under five teachers' charge for our transatlantic adventure. There's nothing like doing a school trip that sets off at 3 am GMT, travels hundreds of miles to London by road, then 3,500 miles to New York, clocking up ten-plus hours of travelling. You cross several time zones and perform some reverse time-travelling, meaning you arrive at 7 am in the morning to start a whole day of tourism with said 50 excitable pupils (none of whom chose to sleep on the plane, meaning that neither could you, because, you know, supervision and all that), even though your body is screaming at you that it is the afternoon and now would be a perfect time for a nap.

At the arrival point of a school trip, especially on a residential, you are all about laying down the new laws of this alien environment. We had covered it all: the itinerary, the rooms situation, the 'under no circumstances should we see any boys on the girls' floor and vice versa on pain of catching the next flight out of NYC' (we love an empty threat, don't we, teachers?). We had discussed the need to see your trip leader at all times when manoeuvring through the city, and we had laid down some heavy rules on how we were to negotiate the subway system, as this was going to be our main way of getting around.

'You're all old enough to take care of your own MetroCard. Cole, are you listening to me?'

'Yeah yeah, Miss. Will, check out that one-armed beggar with the saxophone.'

'Cole, you'd better be listening, as I am not about to re-enact *Home Alone 2* with you lost in New York. If you lose your MetroCard, you will have to use your spending money to buy another.'

'Yeah yeah, Miss.'

I'd made a bet with another member of staff that 'if anyone's going to lose their card, it'll be someone in my group'. Counting out some dollars and setting them aside from the emergency fund for when this eventuality happened, I looked up just in time to see Cole dancing around by an approaching subway train. As the door opened, he started showing off to his friends and jumped on the train and jumped off.

'Cole, get off there! What are you playing at?!' I bellowed, but Cole didn't hear me. He was too busy basking in the glory of the laughter he was getting from his peers. As he jumped on the train for the second time, the doors slammed shut, three times the speed of the tube doors that we were used to in London, and just as quickly as they shut, the train shot off, but not without me being able to see Cole's shocked face before he disappeared into the night.

'Where the hell is that train going?' I managed to get out in a squeak.

'I wouldn't worry too much, Ma'am,' said a native New Yorker, 'the D train will get him straight to the Bronx.'

The Bronx, excellent, what a wonderful place to be struck off the teaching register!

Luckily, I'm not the only one to have had a 'mare abroad, as Ben tells us about his fun in Europe.

Case study: Ben Davies, PE teacher

What a delight to be taking away 35-plus students to the south of France on a water sports trip. Sun, sea and… sensible fun! In our second location near the beach, we were put up in some lovely cabins on stilts, which I found rather amusing at the time, but later discovered exactly why. Despite living in the lap of luxury, the students were camping, six tents per plot. Whilst unpacking their bags, the students were reminded (several times) by the rep to place their bags on the units or their bed cabinets when not in their tents or at night. Another strange instruction given that anyone who has worked with teenagers knows 100 per cent that they prefer to use the floordrobe to store clothes and the like.

We had been having days and days of blazing sun and dry nights, with no inkling of rain whatsoever. Little did we know that just around the corner was one of the biggest storms to break over the summer period. This was not what we had asked for but we were given ample notice by the reps and how to prepare. Shock horror: store your bags on the unit or bed cabinets, the students were reminded again and again and again, but the teenageitis must have affected their hearing and many a bag was still happily stored in the floordrobe.

After a fantastic day banana boating, kayaking and eating a buffet lunch (my favourite activity), we all headed back to our accommodation to freshen up for dinner. This for the boys meant using three cans of Lynx ('Shower in a can, Sir, innit'), putting on a two-day-old T-shirt with minimal stains and using copious amounts of hair gel. For the girls it meant spending 45 minutes doing I don't know what and coming out for dinner looking fabulous.

Remember that warning we were given by the reps? I bet you could close your eyes and recite it word for word by this point: 'When not in your tents, please place your bags on the unit or bed cabinet.' The girls by now had bought into this and had been impressive in their storage of their clothes. The boys again, probably distracted by a wrestle, a bag of sweets and some football chat (perhaps I am being a tad stereotypical, but I overheard them so I know I'm right in this particular case), had ignored all the warnings, requests and reminders and left their items everywhere.

The night came and all was quiet. Everyone was asleep and not a peep could be heard from any tent or cabin when Storm Deidre decided to show up. Thunder, lightning and an exponential amount of rainfall within 20 minutes had turned our plot into a brown lagoon. My colleague who is essentially Bear Grylls shot out of bed and began digging trenches to divert the rain away from the tents. I, on the other hand, took a little longer to rouse but soon realised that the tents had been flooded and the students were getting a tad worried about their items.

As the boys frantically scrambled to pick up their already drenched belongings, alas, it was too late for them and several tents became giant washing machines only without the suds or the clean clothes.

We all had to evacuate our plots and head for the main lodge and all items were to be taken with us. All this at 3 am! We then spent the rest of the night on a rollout mat on the floor. I still think I could have stayed in my cabin as the stilts had provided a clear path for the rain to sweep past us and into the tents. The following day, there was no more rain, and with shrunken clothes, we had our last day on the beach and then headed home.

My tips for your school trips would be:

- Always make sure you differentiate your requests and tasks, and use modelling to help pupils understand what you are looking for.
- Don't assume everyone has understood the instruction just because they are nodding their heads, particularly boys in my experience as they need a lot more coaching.
- Always know what your exit strategy is and have multiple plans to deal with multiple outcomes.
- Use the students in your group to demonstrate good practice. This is particularly useful in mixed-ability groups.
- Discuss personal hygiene with students in a discreet and professional manner, as some can be very sensitive.
- Always travel with Bear Grylls!

Ben Davies is a PE teacher. It has been 12 years since his NQT year and he has the joints to show for it!

An amazing example of how, no matter how much planning you do for a trip, there can always be something to take you by surprise! Though not funny at the time, it's a great thought to be able to look back and smile as you all made it out alive, with or without Bear Grylls.

Plays for the playbook

So, I'm going to step in here and get us thinking about some school trip plays for the behaviour management playbook.

Expectations

From the word go, you need to make your expectations for the trip clear and known, with no ambiguity or wiggle room. Most classrooms in a school have the expectations visible somewhere and this can serve as a reminder to the pupils, but once you are out of school you lose this resource. Some secondary schools still have these in items such as a homework planner, so it could be useful for you to request that they have them on their person as a reminder. Some of the pupils you work with may demonstrate a more challenging persona on trips, so they may need to have this information available to them in a way that they can access quickly and effectively. Some primaries use visual support by creating symbol-based resources, so that children are able to see pictorial instructions and commands. This tactic also works throughout the key stages for certain pupils.

If possible, and if it would be beneficial for identified pupils, see if you can have a run-through of specific aspects of the trip or similar scenarios, for example, a different-style dining room to the school's, and the modelled behaviour you would like to see. This should be done with the identified pupils prior to the trip so that they have further understanding of the expectations. I would always see an activity such as this as important social skills work that should be executed during any additional intervention time that they may have access to, or within PSHE lessons.

Risk assessments are there for a reason

We have probably heard of the freak accidents that have occurred on school trips, and while I am very keen not to catastrophise, I think it is incredibly important to realise that the risk assessments are there to keep us safe and aware. Any setting that accepts school parties is likely to have their own risk assessments in order to support their liability insurance. Take the time to go through theirs with a fine-tooth comb and then think about the areas that you need to add in to personalise it. Include information such as pupils' individual medical needs, but (pertinent to our overarching theme) you should also include details of the behavioural needs of the pupils who will be attending with you. Although it may seem like a daunting thought to bring a child along who has the ability to turn your trip from a smooth-sailing day to chaos, you should already know the pupils and the traits they have prior to the trip, so this will help you to stay one step ahead in the risk assessment process.

Here are some examples:

- **Are they a climber?** Call ahead and see if there are any areas that lend themselves to this and plan to avoid them.
- **Are they likely to abscond to find the local shops, or do they know someone locally on the trip?** This may be too much of a lure for them to stay on task. Finding out this information beforehand gives you the opportunity to put in place restrictions and rules for them to see what the expectations are.
- **Do they have a better relationship with certain members of staff?** If so, are you able to get them on the trip with you for that immediate relationship and interaction in an alien environment?
- **Do they lack basic social skills that could lead them to be abrasive in public?** The use of social stories prior to trips and modelling of positive behaviour in the run-up will allow you to be able to use a common language when on the trip so that you aren't trying to train them on the spot.

Also, never underestimate the importance of being able to deliver a dynamic risk assessment. The ability to assess a situation on sight will allow you to determine if it is in the best interests of pupil behaviour to go ahead with the initial plan. For example, if you arrive at the same time as another school for a tour and you can see that the behaviours between each group are bubbling, can you as the trip leader ask how the tour could be done differently to avoid further interactions with the potential distractions from that school?

Communication is key

It is key to communicate, not just with the venues, the transport or the parents, but actually with the pupils themselves. Providing regular check-in points can promote a feeling of independence (throughout the key stages), but it also limits the amount of time with unstructured interaction. Providing the ability to check in regularly means that you can allocate opportunities to regulate them, especially if they are entering a phase where they are beginning to fail to regulate themselves. The regularity of these check-ins means that you are limiting the time that pupils have to escalate and spiral towards a crisis situation, and you are able to remind them of the steps they may need to take or pre-learnt skills they will need to use to help keep their day successful.

Share the mental load

Voicing the concerns that you may have working with certain pupils outside of the school setting will turn it from a worrisome task to a problem-solving activity. Speaking to the key adults of those pupils for tips and triggers will help you to formulate a more solid plan. Inevitably, they will have the knowledge and skills to come up with scenarios and thought processes that you may not have even considered. It is also always very useful to get a viewpoint that is different from your own. You may be able to discover some of their interests that could lead to a good distraction technique or be an 'in' for them to feel more engaged with the topic and the trip. Try and touch base with teachers who have done the same or similar trips with the same or similar year groups and behaviours.

Have details to hand

Be armed with the facts and plans that you have spent all that time researching, and share them with any adults on the trip. I have seen many handy ways of having key information for a student to hand. These could be as simple as a folder in the bag, or as resourceful as printed business cards with key prompts, buzzword reminders and emergency numbers. When they are needed in a particular moment, there will be no fumble for information, resulting in no time lost when having to deal with a situation.

Know your emergency support network

Have a contingency plan in place with the family and with the SLT back at school, so you know that if you have exhausted all of your options, you are not left without a resolution. Ask for the SLT to support you if that call needs to be made to make a strong decision, such as removal from a trip due to negative behaviour. Don't forget to outline the clear outcomes of the behaviour that could lead to this action for all involved.

Reward system

Before you leave on your trip, if you are aware of motivators within that individual, whether intrinsic or extrinsic, work these into your planning. Perhaps you can walk with a bag of marbles in your pocket and each time you see positive and polite behaviour, the pupil puts a marble into a container for them to count at the end of the trip and convert into house points. Is there a certificate that they can see at the beginning of the day and aim to have their name written on it at the end because of excellent engagement? You can be as creative as the trip offers you to be. Talk with the pupil beforehand and see whether they have anything in mind that they would like to work towards, such as an early lunch pass or first pick at toy time. Rewards do not have to cost money. Your investment in the creativity of rewards is sometimes the only thing you need to spend.

Don't forget to reflect

And after all is said and done, make time to reflect on the day. Everything is a learning opportunity and an experience that you can take forward into your next trip, no matter how disastrous you feel it may have been!

*

I suppose after all this, you're wondering what became of Cole, and whether he is still in the Bronx making his way in this cruel world, busking alongside the one-armed saxophonist. Well, luckily for him (and me), it would appear that he had been listening to our directions after all. He had as good as a dog tag around his neck that was made so he could tell anyone if he was lost where his hotel was, his teachers' names and contact numbers, and the back-up plan. And prompts that if he was seriously lost, he should get help from an emergency service!

Even more luckily for him, he had been seen messing about on the inside of the train by someone who happened to be a high-school teacher, who no doubt could see a version of Cole in one of the kids he taught (pupil behaviour is a worldwide translatable language). The gentleman went over to him, told him to stay by his side and ignore the buskers, and rode the subway with him back to the point where his ridiculous antics had started. I was on the subway platform as the member of staff allocated to be waiting in case he came back to that point. I have never seen a paler, more shamefaced child arrive back on that platform as I did that day. Suffice to say that Cole didn't leave my side for the rest of that trip, partially because I told him not to on pain of death, and partially because I think the things that he saw on the subway that night made him realise that maybe his teacher *did* have his best interests at heart after all!

Reflective space: So... it all went tits up on a school trip

Think about something that went wrong in terms of behaviour on a school trip that you have been on. Perhaps it was your first trip or you'd already participated in several. Maybe you'd even planned it. Note down some key learning points that will help you when it comes to your next trip.

1. What happened?

_____

_____

_____

_____

2. Was this experience personal?

_____

_____

_____

_____

3. How did the incident make you feel?

_____

_____

_____

_____

4. Is there a repeat offender involved in the situation?

_____

_____

_____

_____

5. Were there any catalysts or red flags to the incident?

_____

_____

_____

_____

6. Have you decided to take any additional steps (e.g. call home, detention, involving another member of staff)?

_____

_____

_____

_____

7. Do you feel like leaving the classroom? Why?

_____

_____

_____

_____

8. What's one thing that you would do differently if the same situation were to arise?

_____

_____

_____

_____

Chapter 12

So... you've finally learnt to laugh at yourself

So, we've come to the final chapter. I'm hoping that throughout this journey you've been able to understand that the entire purpose of this book is not to sit here and tell you what to do in terms of successful behaviour management and effective control within our wonderful classrooms. It is, in fact, to get you thinking and flexing your brain, being a reflective practitioner and finding the tools for you to analyse the behaviour you're seeing in your classroom and what you can do about it. And to notice along the way that you really aren't the only one to have experienced these emotions, situations or dilemmas.

The underlying theme and message of this book is that not only are we human, but so too are the pupils we get to work with day in, day out. And along with humans will inevitably come hilarious situations (which may not feel quite so funny at the time). I began this book with the age-old adage of 'Never work with animals or children', and it will never be lost on me how many ex-teachers are now well-known stand-up comedians. There are very few jobs similar to teaching, where your material is essential in whether you sink or swim, your delivery is your tool to keep your audience hanging off your every word, and how if you mess it up at any stage, there will be a heckler waiting to make you pay, so make sure you have an arsenal of responses ready at your disposal, readily chosen, practised and allocated to specific heckler situations.

I imagine that many a teacher's go-to anecdotes at a social gathering are pulled directly from a classroom interaction or corridor run-in, explaining why teachers sometimes gravitate towards other teachers in social settings or, if they have non-teacher friends, are banned from 'talking shop' because the archives are deep to pull from. Although we can get caught up discussing the latest government shake-up, we can always bring it back to an experience that has led us to saying, 'You'll never guess what happened to me yesterday afternoon.'

This is not to say that other professions don't regularly use this saying either. I quite frankly would love to be a fly on the wall of the personal assistants to the rich when they meet up to discuss some of the ridiculous requests that they no doubt have to endure on a daily basis. I will be first in line in the queue for their memoirs. But it's the consistently erratic interventions of children's out-loud thoughts, the impulsive delivery of actions without thought of consequences and, more than anything, the safe environment that school can provide that lead to these interactions. In any place children visit on a daily and regular basis, and where there is regularity and familiarity, there will come the testing of boundaries. They say that a toddler is far more likely to test a parent at home than when they are out in public because of the safe environment and stability that their homelife provides, and I think that this is not dissimilar to the scenario that we replicate in school. There are more opportunities to go for broke with your behaviour when there is a ready-built audience at your disposal, but also when you know the consequences of your actions. Quite frankly, you'll take the detention or the lost breaktime because it's worth it. But learning to smile at these situations when it feels like it's the most mortifying thing, a potential career-ender, or something you really should have thought about planning for, that is a skill that we need to learn to develop over the years, and revisit at every opportunity, especially in the moments when we might question:

'Is teaching really for me?'

What better way to confirm the thought of smiling (not grimacing) our way through our trials and tribulations than to leave you with a few final stories? Let me share with you the moment in my career that makes me laugh the most, and have Heather and Bethan bring it home with two moments that, quite frankly, made me belly laugh.

I used to be a head of house in a school where the other three heads of houses were just as competitive as me, so winning at all costs was important. This led to hilarious (so we thought) videos being filmed every term for the end-of-term assemblies. They were great because they filled up the 15-minute assembly. There were only so many venues that could fit all the houses in, so once a term two of the houses had to double up and go into the hall. This meant no film to kill time. This particular term it was my house, Fire, and Earth house that had to come together, a fierce rivalry.

Because we had half the school in the hall, we knew we needed to keep them engaged, entertained and interested, especially as they were all hyped from it being the last day of term and them being in their own clothes. But we had the harder task, as there was no video.

On each of our prefect teams, we had realised that we had a set of twins, one in my house and one in the other. They were the most amazing boys. They loved basketball, loved science, loved learning, loved going the extra mile and were a genuine pleasure to have around, but if you thought the staff were competitive, the Braxton boys were next level.

I had devised a competition: 'Which Braxton was better?' In hindsight, it was a stupid concept to pit these two boys against each other all in the name of extra house points and supreme bragging rights.

All was going fine. We did a simple press-up competition, 'Who could shout the loudest?' with the pupils voting by cheering, and 'Who could get a member of staff's lanyard the quickest?' with the pupils cheering them on to go faster. Going well, that is, until I sat them down for 'Who could eat a doughnut the quickest without licking their lips?' I learnt in that moment the lengths these boys would go to in order to win, including one turning bright red because they'd nearly choked themselves in the process, and the other being violently sick on the way out of the hall. That doughnut came out practically whole, as well I found out whilst putting the sawdust down! That assembly perhaps would have gone down well if my lack of foresight in hyping up 500-plus children on the last day of term before the second period hadn't led to the most behaviour logs being recorded that day. I riled them up, then sent them onwards to their lessons, further supporting the narrative that some teachers have that we should teach right up until the bitter end and not do activities such as watching a film. Always consider how what you are planning and delivering could have an impact on your colleagues, either because they are teaching them next or because they are in the classroom next door. Paying that courtesy to colleagues could prevent you gifting them a tricky lesson because of what came before.

Anyway, I can laugh about that assembly now because Fire took the win. We all know that vomiting after a food-eating contest is instant disqualification...

Case study: Heather Tucker, English teacher

As Charlie Chaplin once said, 'A day without humour is a day wasted.' I consider humour and laughter essential in my life and I try to ensure they also happen in every lesson I teach. At five foot, I've always had to laugh at myself – even the author of this book refers to me as her favourite PORG (person of restricted growth). I use this to my advantage; I always pick the tallest pupil to do a demonstration at the front next to me, so the class can giggle that a 12-year-old is taller than a 33-year-old. I've dressed up as an Oompa Loompa for World Book Day, and when I was head of year, I took Christmas prizes around to my form classes as an elf.

But we've all had *that* class. The class that makes you feel nervous and dry-mouthed just before teaching them. The unpredictable class that makes you feel like a dreadful teacher, no matter how experienced you are. The class that doesn't laugh with you but laughs at you, and you can't help but take it personally.

10 set 3 were *that* class. They were the notorious 'mean' class of the school and they knew it. I'd tried all the usual techniques to get them on side and none of them worked. The harder I tried, the worse they seemed to get and it had got to that awful 'me vs them' mentality. The lessons were a slog and I was certainly no fun. I nagged, I shouted, I moaned but I didn't get anywhere with them. I'd become *that* teacher whom nobody liked or respected and I was too far in to get out of it.

Picture the scene. It was the last lesson of the day and *that* class were running rings around me. It had got to that point which every teacher has had at least a few times in their career. I had been teaching six years and I had no control whatsoever over the class. None.

At the exact moment when I was considering giving up and sticking my head in the recycling bin until 3.05 pm, one of the feral boys (let's name him Lucifer) decided to roll on the floor whilst swinging his chair in the air and singing, for no explicable reason, 'Flying Without Wings'.

I walked over, squatted down next to him and quietly and calmly asked him to sit back on his chair as his behaviour was unsafe.

He rolled over, smiled sweetly and shouted, 'Shut up, Miss, you dull c**t.' Silence. He knew he'd gone too far and everyone looked at me and waited for my response.

It took all the energy I could muster to suck my bottom lip in and not cry. 'Could you stand outside please, Lucifer?' I asked quietly. After he had left the room, the rest of the lovelies waited with bated breath to see what would happen. Would I scream? Would I cry? Would I shave my head *à la* Britney Spears 2007?

Although I was sorely tempted to do the former, I shut the door, took a deep breath and turned around to face the music.

'I hate that word,' I announced. 'I'm many things, but I'm certainly not dull.' They belly laughed and so did I. It was a turning point for the whole class. It was the first time we'd laughed together and boy did it feel good. I realised that because I had been taking myself so seriously, they had not seen me as a person and therefore had no interest in what I had to say.

Laughter really was the best medicine. 10 set 3 (including Lucifer) quickly became the class I looked forward to having 'bants' with and they certainly never thought of me as a 'dull c**t' again.

Heather Tucker is an English teacher in a secondary school in Wales. It's been ten years since she was an NQT.

I'm with Heather here. I can't think of anything worse than being dull, but if this book has taught us anything it's that teaching is anything but dull! And Bethan is going to bring us home with this in mind for our final case study.

Case study: Bethan Jones, deputy head of maths

The class is finally under control. You're on top of things. A bit of low-level disruption here and there but you've been doing this for almost a year now. You know what to do. You're midway through an explanation and it's going well – they actually seem relatively interested in what the difference between an expression and an equation is! Denis is mumbling to his friend but this isn't an issue. You give him your meanest stare and make your way to the whiteboard to write his name on the warning side, as per the behaviour policy. You're so good at multitasking now you can even write names on the board whilst watching and talking to the class.

You feel the strokes of the whiteboard marker spell D-E-N-I-S. Denis goes red, presumably at the sight of his name on the 'negative' side of the board. The faces of the students in front of you start to change. Some look at the floor, others go a bit red themselves, some have smirks, and the rest look at you epitomising the shocked face emoji. The feeling of dread in the bottom of your stomach that you used to feel most days in your first term of teaching is back again. Do you have something on your face? Perhaps the marker pen has burst on your top? You turn around to see if there's anything on the board and you have your answer.

The stem of your capital D is longer than usual – a mistake in your blind penmanship. A mistake that has caused your D to look more like a P. I think we all know what Denis now reads. Your heart is in your mouth as you turn back round to face your class. You have options: calmly ignore the mistake and continue with your lesson (sensible), sanction those who are smirking (could go horribly wrong), or succumb to the laughter bubbling up inside you (terrible decision).

Unfortunately for me, my inner 12-year-old gave me no choice. When this happened at the end of my PGCE year I could not contain the giggles, and as a result, the whole class erupted in hysterics. It took at least five minutes for them (and me) to calm down and poor Denis's red face may have taken a while to return to its original colouring. But sometimes, you've just got to laugh.

This is just one of many hilarious mishaps that have happened to me on my teaching journey. This one was particularly poignant as it happened just as I felt that I had gained control of this hectic and unpredictable teaching profession. Yes, it may have been better to keep calm and carry on, like I'd been taught to do. However, to be honest, this was much more enjoyable. Building relationships is so important, and whoever said 'Don't smile until Christmas' must have really disliked their classes. Of course you can smile – you've gone into this profession for a reason! You're bound to make mistakes throughout your journey in this job but if you can't have fun, what's the point?

Sometimes it can be challenging to find the fun in your classroom. Not everyone will have classes where they can laugh together. Therefore, my final tip to ensure you can make light of those difficult moments is to foster relationships with your peers, not just your students, so that what may have seemed the most crushing point in your teaching life can later be looked upon in jest with your friends.

No one understands teaching better than a teacher, so make sure you surround yourself with colleagues who bring you up after a bad lesson, not put you down. You need friends to get you through what can be the most challenging (but rewarding) years of your life. You need to find joy in the, perhaps initially, few moments that you can. You need to laugh at yourself.

Bethan Jones is a deputy head of maths and has been teaching for two years since her NQT year.

Reader, after going along on this wonderful journey together through shared times of cringe and 'I should have known betters', dispelling the notion that those who can't, teach, with a little bit of research thrown in to get those brain cells ticking, we've come to the end. Hopefully you're feeling better about the things you've done and you're feeling revitalised to pick yourself up and try again. Whether you're ITT, NQT, starting a new school, or just having a crisis of confidence as to whether you can do this job, I promise you, you can, and the fact that you have stayed reading to this final page tells me that you do in fact want to be in education. My final message to you? Teaching and working with children is hilarious, rewarding, uplifting and sometimes soul-destroying in equal measures, but if you can keep up the humour with a decent plan of action and reflective analysis along the way, you'll have the most incredible career to look back on. I'm only a decade in and I'm already brimming with wry-smile moments to keep me going.

So... feel free to smile, and laugh... way before Christmas!

References

Adelman, H.S. and Taylor, L. (1990), 'Intrinsic motivation and school misbehavior: Some intervention implications', *Journal of Learning Disabilities*, 21, 541–50.

Allman, K.L. and Slate, J.R. (2011), 'School discipline in public education: A brief review of current practices', *International Journal of Educational Leadership Preparation*, 6, (2), 1–8.

Amabile, T.M. and Gitomer, J. (1984), 'Children's artistic creativity: Effects of choice in task materials', *Personality and Social Psychology Bulletin*, 10, 209–15.

Bennett, T. (2017), 'Creating a culture: How school leaders can optimise behaviour'. London: Department for Education, www.gov.uk/government/publications/behaviour-in-schools

Borko, H. and Putnam, R.T. (1995), 'Expanding a Teachers' Knowledge Base: A Cognitive Psychological Perspective on Professional Development', in: Guskey, T.R. and Huberman, M. (eds.), *Professional Development in Education: New paradigms and practices*. New York, NY: Teachers College Press, pp. 35–66.

Brophy, J. (1999), 'Toward a model of the value aspects of motivation in education: Developing appreciation', *Educational Psychologist*, 34, (2), 75–85.

Department for Education (2018), 'Factors affecting teacher retention: Qualitative investigation', www.gov.uk/government/publications/factors-affecting-teacher-retention-qualitative-investigation

DeWitt, J. and Storksdieck, M. (2008), 'A short review of school field trips: Key findings from the past and implications for the future', *Visitor Studies*, 11, (2), 181–97.

Education Endowment Foundation (2019), 'Improving behaviour in schools: Six recommendations for improving behaviour in schools', https://educationendowmentfoundation.org.uk/tools/guidance-reports/improving-behaviour-in-schools

Erden, M. (2008), *Classroom Management*. Ankara: Arkadaş Publishing.

Evertson, C.M. and Harris, A.H. (1999), 'What we know about managing classrooms', *Educational Leadership*, 49, (7), 74–8.

Fabelo, T., Thompson, M.D., Plotkin, M., Carmichael, D., Marchbanks, M.P. and Booth, E.A. (2011), 'Breaking schools' rules: A statewide study of how school discipline relates to students' success and juvenile justice involvement'. New York, NY: Council of State Governments Justice Center.

Holcomb, S. (2016), 'How one middle school cut discipline referrals by 98 percent in just one year', *NEA News*, http://neatoday.org/2016/02/17/middle-school-discipline-referrals

Martin, N.K., Yin, Z. and Mayall, H. (2007), 'The attitudes and beliefs on classroom control inventory – revised and revisited: A continuation of construct validation', *Journal of Classroom Interaction*, 42, (2), 11–20.

Ofsted (2018), 'Ofsted research on lesson observation models', www.gov.uk/government/publications/ofsted-research-on-lesson-observation-models

Ofsted (2019), 'How valid and reliable is the use of lesson observation in supporting judgements on the quality of education?', https://assets.publishing.service.gov.uk/government/uploads/system/uploads/attachment_data/file/936246/Inspecting_education_quality_Lesson_observation_report.pdf

Payne, R. (2015), 'Using rewards and sanctions in the classroom: Pupils' perceptions of their own responses to current behaviour management strategies', *Educational Review*, 67, (4), 483–504.

Piaget, J. (1959), *The Language and Thought of the Child* (3rd edn.). London: Routledge & Kegan Paul.

Salvano-Pardieu, V., Fontaine, R., Bouazzaoui, B. and Florer, F. (2009), 'Teachers' sanction in the classroom: Effect of age, experience, gender and academic context', *Teaching and Teacher Education*, 25, (1), 1–11.

Seoane, M. and Smink, J. (1991). 'Incentives and education: A series of solutions and strategies'. Clemson, SC: National Dropout Prevention Center.

Spaulding, C.L. (1992), *Motivation in the Classroom*. New York, NY: McGraw-Hill.

Vygotsky, L.S. (1978), *Mind in Society: The development of higher psychological processes*. Cambridge, MA: Harvard University Press.

Wong, H.K. and Wong, R.T. (2018), *The First Days of School: How to be an effective teacher* (5th edn.). Mountain View, CA: Harry K. Wong Publications.

Index